CW00495041

Conversations with
MOTHERS AND
DAUGHTERS

CELIA DODD

An OPTIMA book

© Celia Dodd 1990

First published in 1990 by
Macdonald Optima, a division of
Macdonald & Co. (Publishers) Ltd

A member of the Maxwell Macmillan Pergamon Publishing Corporation

British Library Cataloguing in Publication Data

Dodd, Celia
    Conversations with mothers and daughters.
    1. Daughters. Interpersonal relationships with mothers
    I. Title
    306.8'743

    ISBN 0-356-12891-1

Macdonald & Co. (Publishers) Ltd
Orbit House
1 New Fetter Lane
London EC4A 1AR

Typeset in 11pt Century Schoolbook by
Leaper & Gard Ltd, Bristol, England

Printed and bound in Great Britain by
The Guernsey Press Co. Ltd, Guernsey, Channel Islands

CONTENTS

Celia Dodd is a journalist, who regularly contributes to *The Guardian* women's page and *The Independent*. This is her first book.

INTRODUCTION

As a mother of two sons, writing this book has given me more than a few pangs of envy. Talking to so many different women about their experiences, good and bad, transformed an impersonal curiosity about female children into a positive desire for a daughter of my own. It confirmed a painfully obvious fact of life which I had refused to face before I had children, but which began to register when they arrived on the scene — that there's a vast difference in the way women relate to their male and female off-spring.

The difference is not hard to pin down. A son may be everything a daughter can be, and more. But what is always missing is a vital ingredient: the intuitive understanding which can only exist between females. Of course, this affinity can be a source of great tension, even rivalry, as well as a firm basis for mutual support and companionship. None of the women I interviewed had totally trouble-free relationships with their mothers or daughters; indeed many of them had much easier relationships with their fathers and sons. But for all of them the bond between mother and daughter was quite unlike any other.

The nature of the mother and daughter relationship depends on an infinite number of factors, most of which we can't even hope to be aware of, let alone do anything to change. The most significant seems to be the mother's experience with her own mother, and the succession of influence handed down from generation to generation through the female line. Breaking that influence can be a demanding, painful, but often essential process.

These days, we expect to get so much more out of relationships than our grandmothers did; the very word has taken on a new significance in our vocabulary since her day. Nowhere is this more true than in the relationship between mother and daughter. Respect, even awe, have gone out of the window; what is now required is friendship.

It's a tall order. For it cannot be easy to be friends with

someone who is not only several years older, but, no matter how liberal she may be, has been telling you what to do for most of your life. And it works both ways. Recent generations have faced particular problems: it must be difficult for mothers who were not remotely friendly with their mothers to forge a very different kind of relationship with their daughters. Their love for their mothers was often tinged with a strong element of fear, and invariably with respect, but friendship rarely came into it. The absence of a satisfactory role model for the new closeness mothers expect to experience with their daughters can be a major stumbling block.

In many ways, maintaining a distance must have made life much easier: at least you knew where you stood. Now women expect so much that it's not surprising if they get let down. The difficulties that arise between mothers and daughters can almost invariably be traced back to a failure of one side or the other to live up to expectations. Daughters of glamorous career women want a mother who is simply there, while housewives who long for their daughters to find a vocation are disappointed when their daughters think that nothing could be nicer than following in mum's footsteps.

The ideal of a delicious, sisterly intimacy, with mother proffering advice and daughter dutifully accepting it, exists only in the realms of fantasy. All relationships worth their salt have their ups and downs, and there is little point expecting otherwise. Daughters who estrange themselves from their mothers in their twenties often become reconciled when their own children are born, and so on. And like any relationship, that between mother and daughter needs hard work — you can't expect to have intimate chats with a teenage daughter if you never communicated with her as a toddler.

At last the idea that mothers are to blame for everything from delinquency to unhappy sex lives is dying out. Mothers don't need any encouragement to blame themselves for their daughters' shortcomings; from the moment of conception, their lives are plagued with guilt. As Sally says of her teenage daughter: 'I'm not responsible for Polly being so bolshy. I can't take that much responsibility; it's not fair. But I find myself doing it, looking at my friends and thinking how their kids are, and I relate it to them. It's really engrained; it's very difficult to get out of. It's an enormous burden of responsibility.'

Peggy, now in her seventies, takes a more sanguine view of her responsibility for her daughter's upbringing, although at the time she blamed herself when things went wrong. 'Nowadays I think it doesn't make much difference what you do, you do your best and hope it will come out right in the end.'

Guilt among working mothers has almost reached epidemic proportions, and it's not surprising, since so many of today's working women had mothers who didn't work, but devoted their lives twenty-four hours a day to caring for the children. You can't brush off role models like that overnight; it was unrealistic to imagine we could.

What mothers can do is present positive images of working women, and women who enjoy life outside the domestic sphere, to their daughters, so that they have inspiring models to build on. At the same time women who choose to look after their children full-time can do a lot to show their daughters that, no matter what the world may say, women's work doesn't necessarily mean downgraded drudgery — it's the most important work in the world.

It is equally important that the current generation of mothers, whether they work or not, avoid perpetuating the myth of superwoman, a stereotype which, again, exists only in the realms of fantasy. By maintaining a pretence of the all-coping mother figure, women do their daughters a great disservice; it's about time some of the burdens of parenting and housekeeping were shifted onto other shoulders, with no sense of failure. That's easier said than done: many women understandably feel, if mother coped, why can't I? But the chain of role models passed from generation to generation needs to be broken at some stage, and it might as well be now.

There are already signs that lasting change is underway.

The arrival of the 'New Man', much maligned, but bearing up under a barrage of criticism and mockery, is just one. The genuine article can do a lot to change our daughters' perceptions of the world, not only by supporting their partners, but by demonstrating that men aren't all macho, incapable of housework and sadly lacking in the emotional department.

One trend that may have a marked effect on the next generation of daughters is the growing tendency to start families later in life. The implications for both mothers and daughters haven't yet been fully explored. A big age gap between the generations isn't a bad thing *per se*, but there are dangers. For example, women who delay motherhood until their late thirties or early forties may invest too much in the relationship — having put off their emotional life for so long, they're determined to enjoy it with a vengeance. Once again, it comes down to a question of unrealistic expectations.

Of course, it's impossible to generalise. One of the purposes of this book is to avoid that danger, by allowing individual women, who have experienced particular problems or pleasures in their relationships, to speak their minds. And while each woman has a very different tale to tell, common threads do emerge.

Psychological analyses of mother and daughter relationships can be difficult to relate to everyday experience, so I've tried to turn this approach on its head, by taking everyday experience as the starting point. The same rationale lies behind the choice of mothers and daughters. None of them are famous, nor do they have exceptionally brilliant careers; they are 'ordinary' women from all walks of life, often facing extraordinary situations.

The result is therefore a bit like a glorified problem page — although it doesn't only deal with the problematic side of the relationship. One stepmother, who had been at the end of her tether with her teenage stepdaughter, told me how she would scour the problem pages for someone in a similar situation — I hope this book will offer the same kind of help, that shared experience can offer.

1.
THE LONGING FOR A DAUGHTER: BIRTH AND BONDING

'I wanted a soul-mate. I think when boys get married they grow away; part of wanting a female was wanting a friend, and I hope it works out like that.'

Margaret

'It really worries me, the thought of them being teenagers and sleeping with people and getting pregnant, or getting AIDS, but I just feel very positive about having girls.'

Wendy

There are endless popular myths to explain why mothers prefer sons or daughters, which go something like this: boys are nicer, more affectionate, when they're young, but they grow away from you; girls are more independent, and more trouble when they're growing up, but they're better company as adults. What it all boils down to is that the attraction of opposites versus the affinity many women feel can only be possible with a member of the same sex. For many mothers, the latter wins hand down. As Gill, a mother of two daughters, Karen and Katy, who has never had an easy relationship with her mother, puts it, 'There is something about a daughter, I must admit. I feel good that Karen's around; it's a nice feeling. And Katy — there's an understanding there. Even with my mother there's an automatic understanding of how women feel.'

The many different reasons women give for wanting a daughter are rarely logical. As often as not it's a gut response which has its roots in relationships with other women, be they friends, lovers or family. For Wendy, who has two daughters aged 5 and 3, it grew out of a very close relationship with her sister, and from her own marked preference for female company: 'I wanted daughters; I don't like little boys as much as girls. Most of my friends are women; I haven't got anything against men but I find it harder to talk to them. And I suppose I just had this feeling that boys are more difficult to bring up. It's not that I'm into little girls being in frilly dresses, I just had this feeling that I could be friends with my daughters, whereas I'd be less likely to be friends with sons.

'I'm very close to my sister, and not at all close to my brother, though he's only a year younger than me and my sister's eleven years younger. She's one of my best friends really. I think that's got something to do with it; I'm close to my sister and I hope I'll be close to my daughters when they're older.

'When I was pregnant with my first baby, I was desperate for her to be a girl. The minute she was born she was rushed off to have the meconium pumped out of her. There were all these people in the room and I was asking whether it was a boy or a girl. It seemed like for ever before I found out that she was a girl.

'And with the second, I wanted her to be a girl too, but I was quite interested to see what a boy would be like. Once I'd got my girl the thought of not having another one was not so dire. But I've got no desire to have a son.'

For other women, like Helen, who has one daughter (16) and three sons (15, 4 and 2), the attraction of opposites, plus a curiosity about the other sex, is much stronger. She admits that she never particularly wanted a girl, and felt a marked preference for her three sons when they were young children which must have affected her relationship with her daughter. Yet now she feels a much greater affinity with Claudia as a teenager than she does with her sons.

'I always preferred boys so that when I had Gianni I was very pleased. I never felt the same immediate tie with Claudia that I felt with Gianni. I didn't feel at all maternal when she was born, though I did when he was born and I did with the other two boys.

'I tried not to let there be any preference but when I used to give them a cuddle before they went to sleep I would always do it more readily for Gianni than I would for Claudia. I don't think I made it longer or anything like that, I was just aware within myself of the feeling. Perhaps one is harder on a daughter, because being the same sex you expect more from them. You make more allowances for boys. It's not right really. I think with daughters you know how much they're trying to get away with and how much is true. These days I identify more with Claudia than with Gianni, but I don't know if it's just the gender thing — though obviously it's easier to identify with a girl — so much as the fact that he's lived apart from me since he was 7.'

Of course, the attraction of opposites works with fathers and daughters too, which can have a huge influence on the mother's feelings for her daughter. Even if he's not on the scene his presence is felt: the father tends to be idealised, even idolised, usually at the mother's expense. Rivalry between mother and daughter for daddy's attention has been well documented, though it's a rare woman who will admit to feeling this kind of competitiveness. Yvonne was one of the few who said she does have a flicker of jealousy at being usurped in her husband's affections by her 2-year-old daughter, Kirsty:

'The flirting starts incredibly early. Just watching Kirsty and little boys I reckon they become aware of sexual attraction at about 9 months. They know there is a difference between mummy and daddy and they know how to play it. Little boys don't tend to flirt with their mums in that way, they're very cuddly and that's what I feel I miss out on. Kirsty isn't cuddly with me. There was a bit of jealousy initially. Clive always used to call me "little one", and she's it now. When he comes home and says, "How's my little one?" he's not talking about me, he's talking about Kirsty.'

Margaret, whose much-longed-for daughter, Chloe, was born two years ago, after four sons, also admits to feeling threatened by the arrival of another female on the scene, but that it did soon pass. 'When Chloe was born my husband and I stared at each other for a long time. He was holding her, then he passed her to me and she cried. I felt rejected then. I also felt a bit jealous. And having been the only female in the household, I did feel threatened. But those feelings were only momentary.'

Gone are the days when bearing a son and heir mattered — or are they? For Asian women, there are still strong cultural, religious and indeed financial pressures to bear a son. Angela, one of five daughters, says, 'My father never had sons, and everybody pitied him because he only had daughters. I've always felt my mother had pressure on her, that she had to produce so much gold for us and so on.'

Hazel Phillips, author of a guide to choosing the sex of your child, says, 'I do get very depressed letters, mostly from Asian women who don't get their boy. If they don't have a boy, women are often threatened that the marriage will be terminated and the husband will find another wife. All through history women have been blamed for not giving the son.'

In Western families, too, prejudices about girls and boys die hard. I can vividly remember being shocked when, shortly after my first son was born, a young and liberal-minded relative waxed lyrical about the fact that he was male — carrying on the dynasty and all that. The traditional view, and one which persists today, is summed up by Ina, a Glaswegian mother of three who is now in her early seventies. Her first child was a girl, Ann: 'I was pleased to have a daughter but actually I would rather have had it the other way round. Before Ann was born I would have liked a boy, but when it was a girl we were quite happy. I think my husband did want a boy first; most men do.'

Gerda, whose two daughters were born nearly twenty years ago, remembers her husband's disappointment that she hadn't borne him a son. Gerda, not a woman to take such overt criticism lying down, reacted by uniting with her younger daughter against him. 'My first husband wanted lots and lots of children, as long as they were all boys. When I had my first, it was Oh, well, never mind it's a girl, it's the first. But the second one he wouldn't recognise at all. He came to see me in hospital the day I had her and announced that she wasn't his child. He wouldn't take her out in the pram, he would never feed her, he wouldn't cuddle her.'

Such extreme reactions may sound archaic, but a longing for a child of either sex, particularly among couples who have several children of the same sex, will always be very common. Some people try over and over again to get the son or daughter of their dreams. Hazel Phillips believes that 'You don't experience the whole of life if you don't have one of each. Out of 4,000 letters I've had from people, only two wanted another child of the same sex; everybody else wanted the other. My grandmother, who had seven sons, prayed and prayed for a daughter when she was last pregnant and she finished up with twin sons. So I thought I would try and write the book to stop that happening to other people.'

In Hazel's experience, women cite a variety of reasons for wanting a daughter. 'Some women, especially the older ones, look to the future and long for feminine company; others just want a pretty doll to dress up. But if they've got a lot of sons they really want a girl. I think women want boys because of the feeling that their husbands would like a son, but they don't have the same sort of affinity with a boy as they do with a girl.'

Margaret, who was inspired by Hazel's book to try for a girl after four sons, gave birth to her daughter, Chloe, two years ago. Like many of the women who have used Hazel's method, she didn't feel her family was complete until Chloe's birth. 'I wanted a mixed family,' she says. 'I thought it would be good for the boys to grow up with a girl, to be aware of women. Anyway, I wanted a soul-mate. I think when boys get married they grow away; part of wanting a female was wanting a friend, and I hope it works out like that. I think Chloe is lucky, too, to be growing up with boys. She's already aware of her sexuality. Recently she announced when we were walking down the road, "I haven't got a willie, I've got a fanny!"

'I was so sure when Chloe was conceived that she was a girl, though I did try to guard myself through pregnancy in case it was a boy. It was the reactions of other people that grated. There was this patronising attitude: I'm so sorry you had another boy. My mother's reaction when I told her I was pregnant for the fifth time was devastating. She thought it was irresponsible, and that only very stupid people have a lot of children.

'Chloe's birth was totally different to the boys'. It was much slower; the boys were very quick. The day I was having her I had three baths and washed my hair three times. It was delightful, magical.'

There seems little doubt that the circumstances under which women give birth can have a lasting effect on their relationships with their daughters, and that 'bonding', that much-maligned buzz word of the eighties, does pave the way for a good relationship between mother and daughter. The experiences of the women I spoke to were mixed: some women felt that an 'easy' labour, with the baby put instantly to the breast, had cemented a close relationship for life, while others felt more distant from their children who had been born 'easily' than from those who had taken hours of agony, in the most clinical environments, to be born. Either way, most women thought the birth had some effect on the relationship.

Diane, an American living in Glasgow, has three grown-up daughters, two of whom were born in the USA. She believes that the difference in their births has had a lasting effect on her relationship with each child. Perhaps co-incidentally, other circumstances have conspired to emphasise the closeness with her youngest daughter, and the distance from the other two, which began at birth.

'I feel closest to Sarah, my youngest daughter, partly because of the birth. During the births of my first two daughters I was out cold, which was the American way at that time (the sixties). So when I woke up I had a baby, and I didn't see either of them straight away. When I had Sarah, who was born in Newcastle, I was awake at the birth, and I knew immediately that I had a baby daughter. Also I took her home within 48 hours, so I think there was almost an instant bonding between us.'

Gill, whose 24-year-old daughter, Karen, was adopted at 10 weeks, noticed a marked difference in the bonding process with her second daughter, Katy, who was born 19 years later. Gill, who also has two teenage sons, puts it down to the revolution in hospital attitudes in the intervening period: 'You didn't see the babies often then, and they were swaddled. You never saw them undressed. You never held the baby, because they were frightened you might drop it. I was probably looking at my baby more than other people, but those moments were snatched really. It was a very strict regime, so the bonding — like I know it now that I've got a 5-year-old daughter — is nowhere the same, it can't be. I can understand how people end up with the wrong babies.

'When Katy came out of my body she looked as if she'd been here before. I've never felt this about children before. She had an extremely knowing look. She came out and she just looked right into my eyes; she looked grown up already. That was a bit uncanny at the time. I bonded with her better than any of them, because these days so much is done to make that time with the baby easier — it's not whizzed away so you've forgotten what it looked like. It was so precious having this time that when they did take her away I made sure my husband went with her — it was a bit of an animal thing.'

Sally is convinced of the evils of a hospital birth, which have been confirmed by much happier later experiences of labour at home with her sons Edward, who is 12, and George, 8. She traces her difficulties in relating to her teenage daughter Polly right back to her conception, and thinks they were exacerbated by a difficult birth, in hospital, followed by immediate separation and a failure to breastfeed.

Sally looks back on the circumstances surrounding Polly's conception with some regret: she was 18 at the time, and saw pregnancy as the only way she could detach herself from her stultifyingly strict background. She says, with some feeling, 'I feel guilty about Polly's conception, but it was necessary for me to survive.' She pretended that she was pregnant to see how her boyfriend would react, and when he seemed resigned to the situation, she proceeded to get pregnant, with Polly. She left Polly's father two years later, but they are still on friendly terms.

'I feel that the way I had Polly — to trick her into being in a sense — has meant that I've never been able to relate to her at all. It's funny, when I was pregnant I thought she would be a boy; I don't know why. I was surprised when she was a girl, but I didn't mind. I've got drawings that I did when I was pregnant of this idealised toddler and baby that are quite unlike Polly; it's always a boy, and he's always got straight hair.

'I was absolutely devastated when the breastfeeding didn't work. When Polly was born they put me to sleep because my blood pressure was very high, and I didn't see her again for 24 hours. I didn't put her to the breast straight away. It took several days before I could really relate to her, and I was aware of why I felt the way I did, because I'd read all about it and I knew that if there was a period of separation I might feel like that. So I wasn't surprised by it, but it was difficult to cope with.

'There was no one to help me learn to breastfeed, so I struggled on with a book, which said you should only feed every four hours. I'd never seen anyone do it; I think my mother used to go off and do it upstairs. When I decided to feed on demand, the nurses just dismissed me; I got no help at all. To me it was part of being a real mother, being able to breastfeed. I'd always had quite negative feelings about my breasts. In the end I failed, I had to stop feeding her, so my breasts weren't even any good for their bio-logical function. But I don't feel that Polly rejected me.

'I think the circumstances of her birth shaped our relationship, definitely, because I have a much closer relationship with Edward, who was born at home; it was a five-hour labour with no drugs. I find being in hospital very intrusive. Comparing my relationship with Polly with my relationship with Edward and George, I don't have any kind of physical relationship with her, I never have done really, and I regret that but it's something I can't force. She does sit next to her dad and let him put his arm round her, so I feel, O God I've failed at something else, she'll probably grow up maladjusted and it will all be my fault. I think it is hard for a mother and daughter to be physical with each other.

'I never played with Polly, even when she was a small child. It was just the way she was, she never needed anyone to play with her, she had one of those fantasy worlds until she was 12 or 13 which she could always escape into. She never seemed to need anybody to be like a parent to her. She's incredibly independent, she always has been. When I was pregnant with my third child, George, I actually wanted a girl, and I was really fed up that he was a boy. There was a split second when I sat up and saw him between my legs and saw his penis and I flung myself back on the bed, I was absolutely furious. Then, of course, I sat up and fell in love with him.

'I think the reason I really wanted a girl when I was pregnant with George was I really wanted to do it again, I wanted a daughter I could be cuddly with, that I could breastfeed, that I could be closer to. Because even by that time — Polly was 8 when George was born — she was already a little grown-up.

'I've always felt troubled by our relationship. I look forward to her coming home from school [Polly went to boarding school when she was 13; Edward when he was 9], but not anything like I look forward to Edward coming home. With Edward it's almost a physical thing, I almost ache to see him. Tears come to my eyes when I think about him. I want him in the way you want a lover, it's that kind of wanting.'

It's as if the initial separation between mother and daughter has led to a distancing on both sides. Sally's main feeling about Polly is that she's extraordinarily independent, a quality she both admires and regards with suspicion. She says Polly never seemed to need anybody to be like a parent, but elsewhere she implies that perhaps she wasn't ready to fulfil that role, when she says, 'Perhaps I was too young when I had her. I don't feel old enough to be her mother.' To some extent, the daughter's behaviour inevitably takes the lead from that of the mother.

Gerda, now in her early forties, thinks that the closeness which exists between her and her 19-year-old daughter, Rachel, goes back to the womb, but not because the birth was easy and her pregnancy untroubled; quite the reverse. 'There's a very strong bond for several reasons. One is that I nearly lost Rachel several times during my pregnancy. I was in contact with German measles at two months, and my doctor advised me to have a termination but I decided, after much thought, to take that chance. Then my husband threw an ashtray at my stomach. I was a chambermaid at the time, and I started to miscarry at three months, then again at seven months. When she was born she wouldn't breathe, and then she wouldn't feed at all.

'It wasn't a maternal feeling I had, so much as a feeling that you've come this far, you're going to bloody well make it through life. You don't owe it to me but you owe it to yourself. I've always had this feeling about her, that you've come this far, no way am I going to let you go on the wrong side.'

Women who know they're expecting a girl often develop a strong relationship with the baby in the womb; knowing the sex enables them to give shape to their fantasies, hopes and fears for the child. Yvonne's fantasies about her unborn daughter stretched far into the future, and certainly helped her through a long labour. Yet her initial reaction on discovering she was expecting a girl when she got the results of her amniocentesis, was disappointment.

'When the doctor said, "It's female", I said, "Oh", because I wanted a boy. I've always wanted boys; when I was a little girl dreaming about having lots of children they were always going to be boys. Then as I got older I thought a boy would be nice for my husband, for all the traditional, sexist reasons, and because we were only planning to have one.

'Clive was quite pleased that it was a girl, though not for the traditional reasons — supposedly fathers love little girls — but because he felt the pressure on a little boy to be like him would be too great. He's very good at every sport he plays so it wouldn't have been fair if a son had turned out like me because I don't have a sporting bone in my body. The fact that Kirsty's a girl means that if she plays sport it'll be a bonus.

'It took quite a while — a good month or so — to get over the disappointment of hearing it was a girl. I started to think more positively about her after everyone who wanted to know the sex had been told. My mother thought I was a bit weird wanting to know. She said why don't you want it to be a surprise, it's so uncharacteristic of you. My answer was that it could only be one thing or the other so it wasn't much of a surprise to hold out for.

'The baby really did become a little girl as soon as I knew; it wasn't a bump or "the baby" any more. We talked about her, we named her quite early and referred to her as Kirsty. We did an awful lot of planning too: walking down the road one day I decided she was going to marry one of our friend's sons, and thought how it would cement our relationship; it was really ridiculous. Because you know the sex you make amazing decisions, like what school you're going to send her to, how you're going to dress her, how you're going to cope with sex. All the things that are maybes if you don't know — like maybe we won't have to cope with her being promiscuous — become definites once you do. They become people very quickly. But superstition still came into it — I wouldn't decorate her room or buy pink clothes.

'All through the labour it was "Come on Kirsty", it

15

wasn't just pushing to get a baby out. I feel I was very close because it was no longer just a baby, because there was definitely a little girl in there called Kirsty Miles. When she was born there wasn't anything about her that I would have recognised as a baby of mine. She was much much prettier — I know all mums think their babies are pretty, but I hadn't expected her to look quite so lovely, even straight out of the womb all wet and slimy.

'It's very difficult to tell whether knowing the sex made any difference to how instant the bonding was. I really did feel very close to this little girl. I knew what she was, I had given her a name and 50 per cent of wondering what it was going to be like was out of the window. I knew that there were girly traits which I had, and I had a vague feeling that I would recognise these things and know how to cope with them.'

2.
A NEW ROLE MODEL? MOTHERS AT WORK AND THE NEW MAN

'*Although Tom helps look after the children and does the washing and stuff, Polly can look at us and she knows damn well that he doesn't think about the details and that I'm still utterly in control of every little bit of our lives. I hope that things will be different for her, but at the moment it's so tokenised.*'

Sally

'*It suddenly occurred to me that I was perpetuating the dreadful stereotypical mother figure for them, that they might then feel they had to be — and that's not good, it's not healthy.*'

Maeve

For the vast majority of women, the most powerful role model in their lives is their mother. Long before we can talk, or even walk, she presents a strong image of how women should and should not behave. Her example may be so powerful that it can be difficult — some would say impossible — to break away from, of which more in the next chapter.

For most women, too, the mother provides the most enduring example of a woman's place in the world, an image which may or may not be reinforced by other images in the world at large.

In the 'post-feminist' era, the women who have tried to break down the accepted view of women could not be blamed for giving up in despair; over and over again you hear women complaining that, no matter how hard they've tried, their sons want to be Superman and their daughters want to be Snow White. Before they had children, goes the complaint, they thought sexism was all to do with upbringing; now they know better, it's nature, not nurture.

It's hardly surprising, since the version mothers and fathers present to their offspring in an attempt to promote a non-sexist view of the world is rarely backed up by what children see all around them. No matter how often you tell your daughter she can be a managing director or a tractor driver when she grows up, she won't believe you if she doesn't see any proof, if all around her she sees women, be they mothers, nannies or childminders, staying at home to do the caring work. And why should she play with a football or wear trousers when the images of girls all around her insist that they like playing with My Little Pony and want to look pretty?

But the battle's not lost yet. The idea that mothers have a right to some sense of identity outside the home, as well as financial independence, is finally beginning to sink in. And of course, it will be positively encouraged as the need to get women back into the workforce to make up for the diminishing numbers of school leavers becomes more urgent in the nineties. The problem for working mothers is that the lessons learnt in childhood die hard; — it's difficult to believe in your heart of hearts that young children don't need their mothers 24 hours a day if that's what you've always been told, and if your own mother dedicated herself to you. The result is, inevitably, guilt. It's almost impossible to find a working mother who has never tussled with this gut-wrenching emotion.

But as more and more women combine work with motherhood, so more and more daughters will see that it's possible, and believe it. The accepted view that women who are successful outside the home take the lead from their fathers is slowly but surely being overturned; future generations will grow accustomed to seeing their mothers as pillars of strength in the world as well as in the family.

At the same time men, at long last, are finding that they enjoy being involved in the caring role which was traditionally the preserve of mothers, that even changing nappies and getting up in the middle of the night can pay huge dividends in terms of involvement and affection. But the 'New Man' is a much maligned phenomenon, and it's not hard to see why — the evidence suggests that even the most helpful partner still has a lot to learn.

Sally's exasperation with the state of things is fairly typical. Her husband, Tom, does his fair share around the house, but Sally remains frustrated by a fundamental difference in attitude, and the fact that her teenage daughter, Polly, is aware of it. While women think about domestic details a lot of the time, planning, and taking steps to avoid minor disasters, men simply don't. They may help with the housework, but when it comes to having the gym kit ready on the right day, or making sure their child has a present to take to a party, they're useless by and large. However infuriating this inability to get bogged down in the drudgery of everyday existence is for their female partners, it must be a great strength for those who operate predominantly in the working world. If nothing else, it means their minds can focus more readily on one thing, rather than fifteen, at a time, which will always remain a problem for working mothers.

Sally says, 'Although Tom helps look after the children and does the washing and stuff, Polly [who is 16] can look at us and she knows damn well that Tom doesn't think about the details — like buying the washing powder — and that I'm still utterly in control of every little bit of our lives. I hope things will be different for her, but at the moment it's so tokenised. I know so many men who do their bit like Tom, but they don't have it on their minds all the time. I begin to wonder if it's biology.' As far as Sally's children go, she says, 'Polly and Edward disprove the theories. Polly is powerful and independent, while Edward is softer. I can see more harm in my boys trying to be macho than in Polly trying to be feminine.'

That's a view which is shared by the Forster family, where the blurring of the roles has gone a step further. Wendy's two daughters, Emily (5) and Alice (3), have a rather different view of male/female roles than most children. For Wendy has one of the best childcare arrangements possible: her husband Dave stays at home to look after the girls. As she says, 'I've never had any of the problems about leaving my children with somebody I don't know.'

It's sad that, even in the enlightened nineties, their solution to the knotty and costly problem of childcare is so exceptional. What is interesting about Dave and Wendy's arrangement is that while the children see their father in a nurturing role, they rarely see him do all the things a mother would traditionally do, because he doesn't do any housework. So although Wendy goes out to work full-time, the girls still see her — or the cleaning lady — doing the household chores. And because he regards looking after the children as a full-time job in itself, he makes sure that he is free from the distractions which most mothers, whether they work or not, are plagued by — they're always trying to do two things at once. In many ways, Dave's role is like that of a nanny — someone whose job is to look after the children with a minimum of household chores.

A man, like a nanny, is more likely to treat childcare as a professional job. While most women might feel they had failed if they couldn't cope with the cleaning — after all, their mother managed — a man is more likely to do something about it, if he can afford to, that is. Sadly most women couldn't behave like that even if they tried because their role in the home has been all too clearly defined by their own mothers.

Wendy explains how the arrangement came about in the first place: 'It was a natural assumption that Dave would look after the kids. For all the time I've been with Dave I've been working full-time and for a lot of the time he's been unemployed. I've always controlled the finances;

he didn't know much about the money side.

'Dave and I are quite different with the girls. If Alice is naughty, Dave is much stricter with her. If he tells them off, they come to me for cuddles. That's quite difficult because I've got to be careful not to undermine what he's doing. Usually he explains things to them in a really nice way. I'm not as patient with them as he is. Sometimes it makes me feel a bit inadequate because I think I am too soft with them. I suspect that if I didn't have Dave's model around I'd slip into being too soft. I tend to try and take the easy way out; he won't give in, whereas I always do for an easy life.' (In this respect Wendy has a lot in common with many fathers, who indulge their children at weekends to the irritation of their wives.)

'I'm much more practical, so if I'm around with the kids I'm often trying to do other things as well, like cleaning up the house, doing washes, gardening and all those jobs. Dave doesn't even try to achieve any of those things; he devotes himself to the children, and because he's creative he does some wonderful things with them.

'If I was at home with the kids I would have something set up every afternoon, and a group of women I did things with, whereas Dave prefers to be on his own with them. He also has this attitude that they're going to have a really great day together — the good fun probably consists of going to the playground and Tesco's — whereas I don't approach it in that way, I get tense and distracted by other things.

'When they're older I think their view of things will be different as a result of Dave looking after them, since what they observe all the time is very different from what most children see, because Dave does most of the caring. Mind you, they don't see him doing the washing and all the other jobs. It would be absolutely hopeless expecting Dave to clean the house in the week so we have a cleaner and a dishwasher. And until he learned to drive recently I did all the shopping.'

Pippa's mother, like Wendy, was the breadwinner in the family; and like Wendy, she took charge of the family finances. Her influence has left its mark on Pippa, who is now 29; her mother is 69: 'I've never believed my place is in the home. I've always felt that I should work and I value that — it's been quite liberating really, right from the start. She used to talk about what kind of careers were open to me, and there was quite a lot of emphasis on that, even after my son was born when I was 17.

'Mum worked all my life. She had to because dad was ill so she really did the only thing she could. She was a nurse and did night duty so that she could be around during the day. She didn't get much sleep. And she never got in the mess that I get in. Looking back on it, it's quite impressive what she managed to do.'

But at the time Pippa wasn't so impressed. 'I would say things like "What kind of housewife are you? — my friends don't have to go through this" when my ballet things weren't cleaned and ironed. And she would just go off; when I was doing my O levels she just left for two weeks because my sister was having problems with her daughter. I got home from school and there was this note saying, "Gone to London to help J. Dad's very ill so you'll have to be very responsible." So while everyone else was swotting and having supper brought up to their bedrooms I was looking after dad. I can see myself going along the same lines though; I think I already do it with my eldest son. But it doesn't fit with my ideal picture of what mothers should be like.

'I've always seen my mother as a strong person. She held the family together. It's ironic that you can admire that strength on the one hand but that was the problem, the fact that she was domineering. She walked all over my dad. But then she'd seen him through alcoholism, you could see why it had happened. She had to learn to cope. He was hopeless with money, so that's why she ended up earning the money and dealing with all the accounts. She even gave him pocket money. It must have been difficult for her, because that didn't comply with her idea of what men should be like — head of the household, strong and macho. It was definitely a matriarchal set-up; my father featured so little, he was so insignificant.'

Although she obviously admires her mother's strength, Pippa admits that as a girl she held a quite different image of motherhood close to her heart; it's an ideal which she has found hard to shake off. 'From the age of 8 to 11 I went to a school in a different part of the country, so I lived with my best friend. Her mother really took the place of mine. That's who I think of as my mother for those years. She was a farmer's wife; she was up at 5 o'clock in the morning and when you got up everywhere was spotless, she was dressed and made up, hair done, with a cooked breakfast on the table. That's the picture I have of the perfect housewife and mother. It was like one big happy family, but when the crunch came she wasn't someone I could talk to.

'When I went back home there was no relationship there, obviously, because it wasn't being fostered. I was really detached. In a way I value that because I don't relish the idea of being wrapped up with my mother all those formative years; I think it was quite healthy.'

But combining work with motherhood is not right for everyone. The trouble is that it's rarely a question of choice; for many women working it is a financial necessity. Diane, a 50-year-old American who has three grown-up daughters, one living in the United States, and two [Vicky, 20, and Sarah, 18] living near her in Glasgow, looks back on her life as a working mother with some regret.

'From the time Sarah was about 6 months old I worked at different things. At first I was training to be a buyer at a store in Newcastle and I had a nanny for Sarah and Vicky, but I realised that full-time work was too much. I missed a lot of important things about Sarah. She was quite interesting to watch at play. She would play a lot with dolls and make them libraries; there was a lot of imaginative play, which was like me as a child. But my husband was doing a second degree at university and we really needed the money so I got a part-time job, but I still felt, especially with Sarah, that I was missing things — first steps, first words and all those things.

'I have mixed emotions about women working when their children are quite as young as that. We can't assess how a tiny child would feel but I felt guilty and I felt I was missing out on things that I wanted to see. I never worked full-time after that first experience because I felt that was not a healthy thing for a mother to be doing. I did it and it seemed to work out well and I liked having the money, but the more I worked the more I thought I couldn't stay home all the time, although originally I don't think I felt that.

'Sarah seemed to accept the fact that I worked, although quite a few of her friends at that time didn't have working mothers. I think now she'd think it was odd if her mother didn't work. Now, with Sarah going off to university, which means all my children are grown, I'm quite glad to have something to do. I can't imagine being a woman alone just doing housework or some little hobby — I wouldn't like that.'

Sarah is evidently very proud of her working mother: 'Deep down I've always felt that mothers should be able to work. When I was younger I thought it was terribly boring that some of my friends' mothers were housewives — my mum had a proper job. But then she's never had one of these jobs that's 9 to 5, she usually gets home at about 3 pm. Perhaps if she'd had a job that meant she didn't come home till late in the evening I might have been more resentful of the fact that she worked.

'The only time I ever wished my mum was more homely was when I was a little bit younger. She doesn't cook and I wanted her to make a cake for me. I saw other people with their "proper" mothers and mine was different. But I wouldn't have any other mother — she's more interesting than most people's mothers.'

Yvonne went back to full-time work when Kirsty was 6 months old. Unlike Diane, she has no qualms about working, and few difficulties in conceding her role to the nanny who takes her place and spends more time with Kirsty than she does. Yvonne is concerned about sexism, and has made tentative efforts to provide Kirsty with positive images of women, but like so many mothers she feels baffled by what appears to be inherent girliness. At the same time she's aware that the mother-father roles in their family are a pretty traditional example for Kirsty to follow.

'I don't feel I'm missing out; having just had a three-week holiday with Kirsty I've got a fair idea of what time is like with her. I sometimes feel I'm missing out on my ideal of what motherhood is about — which is this idyllic day when you have quality time with your child and you sit and paint and draw and they look and appreciate and copy, but I know that most days aren't like that — they're one in ten. I know my ideal of motherhood is a dream.

'When I first went back to work it was other people's hang-ups I found most difficult to cope with. It was other people who said if I were in your position I'd feel this or that or the other, and I felt guilty because I didn't feel like that. After a couple of months I got used to it and learned how to handle it.

'I didn't go through pangs of guilt, but then she never cried after me or anything. I suppose if she had I would start thinking I was abandoning her. Sarah, the nanny, arrives every morning and quite often I don't even get a goodbye from Kirsty.

'I found Sarah when Kirsty was 14 weeks old. I'd be dishonest if I said I didn't get jealous, mostly about silly things. For example, we spend a fortune on clothes for Kirsty. We go to this twee shop in Richmond twice a year and kit her out in one or two wonderful outfits. If I come home and see something new in the wash I'll be disappointed, because I wanted to be the first to see her in that — it's silly. I don't say anything because it would be petty.

'I didn't get upset feeling I'd missed out on the first word or the first step, but I think that is because Sarah is not one to brag about what Kirsty's done. She'll let me say to her, "Oh, I see she does so and so", and she doesn't say, "Oh yes, she's been doing that for days" — she just says, "Yes, it's good isn't it?" Sarah plays me very well, she's sensitive to my needs.

'It's quite evident that Kirsty gets confused when we're both around. She wonders who to go to. If it happens for any length of time, like a couple of hours, it really gets quite confusing. And if she makes the decision to go to Sarah when she falls over or something, then I do get the odd twinge.

'Circumstances force me into the authoritative role with Kirsty, because my husband works late, so he doesn't see as much of her during the week as I do. As far as that goes, we're quite a traditional family couple, it's me that does the most for Kirsty, and it's a convenient excuse to say that circumstances don't permit him to take a bigger role in changing nappies, bathing her and so on — to be honest, if he was around more I'm not sure it would happen. But we do take turns to go to her in the night.

'I believe in all things in moderation. She's definitely being brought up in a house that's non-sexist because Clive does most of the cooking and she sees both of us cleaning and painting and wallpapering. But I've never stopped people giving her dolls or anything like that.

'There are all sorts of things that I think are inherent; there is no reason why she does a load of things that are very girly — she won't have seen me do them, although she may have seen Sarah. I'll talk to her about sexism when she's old enough to understand what it is we're trying to teach her.'

Maeve, a lesbian mother of two teenage daughters, has strong views on stereotyping, which she thinks is partly a reaction against her own upbringing. She also puts her finger on one of the key issues for working women in the nineties, when she says she wants to make sure that she doesn't present her daughters with a role model of a super-woman, a stereotype which it is impossible for her to live up to and for them to follow. Women do their daughters a great disservice if they perpetuate this modern myth.

When Maeve's daughters were small, she was forced to work for financial reasons, although she would have preferred to have stayed at home looking after them. 'I tried to organise work to avoid leaving the girls. When the first one was about a year old I started doing a part-time job as wages clerk which I could do at home. And I used to sew and knit and tie-dye things to sell and did a lot of baking for a health-food shop. In desperation to make ends meet I've been an artist's model and a waitress.

'When they were small I enjoyed being with them a lot. I got really into early childhood development. I've still got all the journals I wrote about it. I suppose in lots of ways I was atypical, but I think that was maybe partly to do with being very young. I hadn't had a career, I hadn't any burning ambitions to be doing anything else, I didn't feel deprived of the world of work. I felt really awful about having to go to work full-time when the younger one was 3.

'At the time I knew a lot of women were very fed up about having small children at home because I was in touch with a lot of mothers through playgroups and so on and I used to feel quite embarrassed because I was enjoying my children and a lot of them were finding it drudgery and dreadful. So my consciousness was quickly raised as to it not being right for large numbers of women.

'I'd always been quite a solitary person, able to amuse myself, so being at home with young children was fascinating; here were these two small things doing all sorts of interesting things. It also gave me a chance to think and write and do things I felt like doing. It sounds idyllic, but there was obviously nappy washing and boring, depressing things to do as well.

'I don't think I had any particularly well worked-out theory or anything, it just seemed really crazy to make girls do one thing and boys do another. I think I had felt that when I was little, with a great deal of resentment about the way my brother got taught. He would get taken down to the cellar to do woodwork with my dad while I was supposed to enjoy washing up. My parents wanted me to achieve things, but the ambitions they had for my brother were more adventurous — they wanted him to be a journalist. My father had this whole thing about women needing to be protected by men. In my mother he chose a woman who needed a lot of looking after. I had this very distorted picture given to me by my parents of how all the strength was in one department and all the weakness in the other, and so I was totally out of touch with (a) my strength and (b) my weakness.

'When my elder daughter was 5 and said she wanted woodwork tools I took her seriously and we went and got proper, good quality tools and a bench for her to work at. Now she's quite critical and says things like, "You only want me to be an engineer because I'm a girl" — it's turned round on its head.

'I deliberately wanted them to be at co-ed schools right the way through. Although there is some evidence that shows that girls supposedly do better at single-sex schools I just felt that, since we're a single-sex family, if they never meet the other lot they might have all these delusions and fantasies about what boys are. That's what happened to me. I was at a girls' grammar school where we all had hallucinations about what boys were like. I'm sure that's why I ended up getting married so young.

'I've always tried to teach them that every human being is worthwhile and valuable in themselves. Even children of 3 and 4 can learn about not hurting people and being considerate. I find it much harder to try and see myself as separate from them and to get them to see me as someone they should be considerate of. It's something I've worked on with the help of a therapist in the last couple of years, that it's actually all right for mothers to have needs. I think that's quite an important issue, because at one time I would be rushing round doing all the washing up and the cooking and the washing and the shopping and stuff, and it suddenly occurred to me that I was perpetuating the dreadful stereotypical mother figure for them, that they might then feel they had to be — and that's not good, it's not healthy. I still feel I'm involved in some sort of learning process myself, of discovering that I don't have to strive to be that kind of superwoman and I don't want them to feel they have to be either.'

3.
MOTHER'S INFLUENCE: BREAKING THE PATTERN

'I think it's impossible not to repeat mistakes, however aware you are, because there's underlying stuff that one isn't aware of that still comes through. I think the whole of my upbringing of my daughters has been a reaction against my own upbringing.'

Maeve

'I used to be in awe of my mum. Even when I was married I felt as if she was still behind me, she could still tell me off. She used to get really mad with us when we were pregnant. She used to say "I don't want you to make the same mistakes as I've made."

Norma

'You're getting just like your mother' is still a common insult much favoured by husbands, who recognise an Achilles' heel when they see one. For most women, the idea that they're becoming like their mothers is disconcerting on several levels. Even a woman who likes and respects her mother doesn't want to be a replica of her; it's essential to our sense of ourselves as individuals that we make some sort of break with our earliest and most influential role model.

There are other reasons which make women feel uncomfortable at any suggestion that they're like their mothers, and which go far beyond the generally accepted idea that women are horrified by the thought of being as old, or as old-fashioned/crabby/intolerant/boring/eccentric as their mothers. Of course, intimations of mortality must come into it — no one likes to think that one day they'll be as old or as set in their ways as the previous generation. It's particularly hard for women to accept the fallacy of the notion, so strong during the hard-done-by teenage years, that when we're mothers ourselves, we'll be much more understanding, we'll remember what it was really like to be young. Growing like mother, for many women, means growing away from that adolescent ideal, and towards intolerance.

Many women, too, express their separateness from their mothers by a conscious attempt to do things differently, so naturally they don't like to think that in spite of all their efforts, their lives and their personalities have turned out to be remarkably similar. The mothers I interviewed said almost unanimously that they wanted their daughters' upbringing to be very different to their own. Often this wasn't a direct criticism of their mothers, so much as an awareness that circumstances had conspired to make things difficult for her, either financially, emotionally, or both.

It's also almost a survival instinct to want to improve things for the next generation, however difficult that may be. Maeve says, 'I think it's impossible not to repeat [mistakes], however aware you are, because there's underlying stuff that one isn't aware of that still comes through. Sometimes that's a source of great sorrow; it just seems really commonplace that every human being would want to try and improve its own situation for its offspring, but at the same time have difficulties about that.

'I think the whole of my upbringing of my daughters has been a reaction against my own upbringing. And I think my awareness of how much that has been the case has increased over the years.

'One of the reasons I wanted to have a baby so early was because I wanted to guarantee the birth would be easy, because all my early childhood my mother, who was 32 when she had me, had gone on and on about how I'd ruined her figure and what a dreadful birth she'd had. She had quite a serious psychiatric breakdown when I was born and was sent to psychiatric hospital for a while.

'It was like my bid for sanity and a healthy adult life to plunge into motherhood early. And it worked — I had *the* natural childbirth, it was what they call a spontaneous delivery.'

Women constantly speak of wanting their daughters' lives to be different from their own, at the most basic level — 'I hope she'll travel more than I did,' 'I hope she'll be better at music than I was,' 'I hope she'll be more sociable because I've always been a wallflower,' 'I hope she'll have a brilliant career because I've always been a housewife.' It can be seen as a desire for vicarious experience as well as a natural instinct for some sort of progress. Some feminist mothers have an optimistic vision of the future which makes some sense of their own struggle. Yvonne says of her 2-year-old daughter, Kirsty, 'The theory is that there will be no avenues that won't be open to women by the time she grows up. Hopefully things that our generation have worked for will be a reality for her and she'll be able to do most things she wants to. I'd like Kirsty to take every opportunity she gets because I didn't.'

One of the most poignant remarks came from Karen, who is 27 and has three daughters of 11, 4 and 2: 'I hope my daughters don't make a mess of their lives like I have. I just want the best for them, like any mother. More than anything I want them to enjoy life before they get married and settle down; I don't want them to have children young like I did; I'd like them to see a bit of the world and get a good job.

'I'd like them to be brought up the way I was when mum and dad were together. I'm strict with them. I don't want them to have the upbringing I had when mum and dad split up. I don't want them to have that much freedom. But it is hard on my own, being mother and father to them.'

Karen was by no means unique in hoping that her daughters would have children later in life than she did. All the women I interviewed who had had their first child in their teens made it very plain that they hoped their daughters wouldn't do the same.

Heather, 42, was brought up by her stepmother, who by Heather's account was in the classic 'wicked stepmother' mould of fairy tales. Heather has worked hard to make sure that her 17-year-old daughter, Joanne, will have a very different kind of life, by making sure that she gets the education she never had.

'I was always getting good hidings from my stepmum, and I had to do all the housework. I was 21 when I left home, because in those days girls didn't get flats like they do now. The day I left she gave me a good hiding, when I was 21! If cruelty to kids was then like it is now she would have been had up.

'I wanted to give Joanne a different life. That's why I like her going to college. I work in a mill and I wouldn't want her to do that. I never went to school half the time; I used to sign my own reports and things like that. I was never encouraged to try at school — when you left, you went to work and that was that. I would never like Joanne to have a life like that, never. That's why I want her to leave home. I'd hate it if I thought she was staying here because of me. I want her to have her own life. That's what it's all for, isn't it?'

If everyone is trying so hard to break with established patterns of upbringing and behaviour, why do so many women's lives resemble, if not their mother's, then their grandmother's or even great-grandmother's? The likeness manifests itself in different ways, some obvious, others not — the number of children they have, and the age they have them, the age they get married, whether they combine work and motherhood, and so on. This can even be the case with daughters who have been separated from their mothers, like Gill and her daughter Karen, who she gave up for adoption twenty-four years ago (see Chapter 8). Gill says, 'When I first saw Karen's photograph album

I had to close the book because I felt sick. There were some very similar things in our lives. Her adoptive mother looked like my mother, who looked like a very stiff person. Looking at the little child's face was just like looking at myself — that really took the stuffing out of me.'

Of course, there are other similarities which are more obviously the result of influence — the way women bring up their children, for example, or the way they behave towards husbands and lovers. Women's relationships with men are often almost repeat performances of their mother's relationships with men. Jane says, 'I've never known what I really wanted to do in life, and my mother never knew either. And in relationships with men we have an awful lot in common, a total disaster every time.'

Maeve gets close to the truth when she talks of 'under-lying stuff that one isn't aware of'. Patterns of behaviour are passed down from generation to generation in a sequence of influence which it is virtually impossible to break. The terrible dilemma is that if women try to, by reacting against their mothers, they are still perpetuating her influence. However, that's not to say it isn't worth a brave attempt! Women will always try to break away from their mother's influence — most particularly in their relationships with their own daughters.

Roberta, who is in her mid-forties, and was brought up in Glasgow and the suburbs of London, was particularly keen to make sure her three daughters' lives were free from the financial difficulties and the unbending rules and prejudice that blighted her own teenage years.

'My mother was a very strong personality. My father was an invalid and he didn't really feature in the family. He just sat in the corner and he was just there, he didn't enter into the conversation. My mother made all the rules, she was very strict. My mother didn't like my boyfriends because she didn't like Catholics, people who lived in council houses, she had a whole list of things she didn't like and because my husband was none of these he was all right.

'I got married and moved away, so she didn't really see my children that often. She really didn't understand how I was bringing them up — it was a different world to her.

'It was a conscious decision to bring them up differently. I felt we had had a very unhappy childhood and I was determined that we wouldn't have the same set up. My teenage years were very difficult, because of the lack of money, a mother who was very tired and under great strain. I think I had the easiest time, being the third daughter; the others blazed the trail. But if I was five minutes late home, if the bus was late, there would be a terrible row. Now I'm in a similar position myself I can see what my mother went through, but of course at the time you don't.'

The extended family, which everyone looks back on with such nostalgia these days, did have some drawbacks, not least the fact that it could be virtually impossible to escape from a mother's influence. In those good old days it was more usual to live with your parents, or have your widowed mother to live with you. She was there to see you following in her footsteps — or not, as the case may be — and to criticise the way you treated your husband and children. Of course, there were undeniable advantages in having someone permanently on hand to look after the children, as Ina, now age 73, found. When Ina was first married, the young couple stayed with her widowed mother, and when her first two children, Ann and Tom, were small they moved to a tenement in Glasgow and mother came too. She lived with the family until she died eighteen years ago at the age of 86.

Both daughter and granddaughter remember her as a strong personality, who 'always seemed old'. A matriarch of the old style, she dominated the household and had a lasting influence on the way family affairs were conducted and on the future of her granddaughter, Ann, in particular. In this respect, Ann's mother regrets her inability to contradict her mother's strong views. Granddaughter Ann takes up the story, followed by her mother:

'Sometimes my husband says I'm getting like my grandmother and I don't like that. I'm a terrible pessimist; I'm always prepared for everything to go wrong. My mother's not like that but my grandmother was dreadful.

'I was never really alone with my mother unless we went shopping or something. Mum never said anything about her mother being around but I think she must have got fed up. You accept these things when you're children, but looking back she must have got fed up. I think granny must have had agoraphobia because she never went out. She was a bit disapproving and very old-fashioned and there were things you knew she would make a fuss about if you came out with them, so I kept quiet when she was around.

'I was always sorry that I hadn't gone on and done some sort of degree. I wasn't encouraged to, although my brother did. I think my parents felt they couldn't afford to have me go on to university. My father worked in the shipyard and my mother worked part-time. Also they didn't really think that girls should go on. I think my mother regrets that now. And, of course, granny was there, who completely disapproved. She didn't think girls should be educated at all — she thought they should leave school as soon as they could and get a job to support the household.'

Ina, Ann's mother, fills in the background: 'Ann has always been matter of fact, always accepting things and making the best of them. I'm like that — maybe too much so. I always feel I should have been more ambitious for myself and for Ann. I'm always sorry that Ann didn't go to university. Being the eldest we had to have her working.

'And my mother, who had quite a strong personality — stronger than mine or my husband's — thought Ann should go out and work. I don't think she would have felt the same way if Ann had been a boy, although she was quite a feminist for that time, and felt women should have a good say in what was happening in the world. She had left school at 13 herself and she resented it; she felt she could have done better for herself, but her father was a tailor and she went into the family business to sew which she never wanted to do.

'Her living with us did put a strain on the family, up to a point. In other ways it was helpful. We had a built-in babysitter, she did all the cooking and she helped with the children. Quite often it was what granny said that went, rather than what mum or dad said. She would say, "You shouldn't let them do that — they should be made to do this or that." Mostly I would just take it and say nothing but there would be times when I got edgy and irritable. Looking back now I sometimes think I took it out on the kids; when she got on to me, I would get on to them. Now my husband does say I'm getting more like my mother every day.'

The generation of women who are now in their fifties and over tended to have a more formal relationship with their mothers than is the case today. Then, the element of awe, even fear, was much stronger, and there were many more taboo subjects. This kind of influence, based on fear, is hard to escape, though many women do manage to create a quite different relationship with their own daughters.

The more relaxed attitude which has tended to develop between parents of middle-age and their children is evident in Alison's close relationship with her elder daughter, Tracy, which is quite different to the distance which has always existed with her own mother. Yet she never made a conscious effort to build a different kind of relationship, and the fact that Alison and her younger daughter are estranged tends to support her feeling that it was more by luck than judgement.

It's ironic that Alison's experience of being the black sheep of the family when she was in her twenties has been repeated by her younger daughter, Michelle. Just as Alison's mother ostracised her from the family when her marriage broke down after a week, and refused to speak to her for nearly two years, so Michelle has been ostracised from the family by her mother.

Although Alison was prepared to challenge her parents' authority on the much more serious issue of breaking up her marriage, it's clear from the way she talks about her sense of duty towards her husband that she accepted without question the model set by her mother, of the wife serving and supporting the breadwinner. Alison still goes in to see her mother, who is 83 and lives with her younger daughter, every day.

'To me, my mum was mum and she still is, there's lots of things even now — and I'm 50 this year — that I could not talk about or say in front of her, but Tracy and I can talk about anything.

'I would never talk to my mum about my husband, for example. I would go round there and say he's got the hump tonight, but I would never tell her what he'd actually said. She'd most likely want to interfere anyway, she's that type. If I'd told her some of the things he's called me in the past, she'd have gone absolutely mad. I'd never have spoken to her about lots of things, about how I run the home, money, how much money he gave me. Tracy can; we can be in the house for 24 hours and not run out of something to talk about, we just keep chatting and chatting. With Michelle, my younger daughter, I always had to try to get a yes or no, and that's how I was with my mother really.

'Now I find that I'm trying to explain things to my mother, instead of my mum explaining things to me. She doesn't understand about my daughter and her boyfriend living together, she can't understand people having a white wedding if they've lived together or if they've had a baby. It's so hard when you've got a big generation gap.

'She was one of those mums who is brought up to believe that life was for her husband, she never went out to work ever. The kitchen sink was always where she should be. Her life was just bringing us children up, she never had any money even for a cup of tea. She's never gone anywhere, she's never been to bingo. When my dad went 29 years ago, she was completely lost.

'I never worked when the children were small and I've only ever worked in the school hours. I suppose I'm a bit old-fashioned in lots of ways, but the two children [Alison's grandchildren, who live with her] do know that their grandad comes first. Like when I'm doing dinner or making a drink he gets his first. I can't help it, it was something right from the word go, when I had my own children. If Frank walked in from work and I was doing anything with them I would stop and get his drink, make sure he was comfortable and then go back to the children. I never made him wait, although he never demanded it, mind you. And when he was still working, the housework had to be done during the day, he would never allow me to iron in the evening.'

Like many women during the war, Norma's mother brought her children up single-handedly for many years while her husband was away in the army. Like Alison, Norma's overriding feeling about her mother was respect, tinged with fear of her disapproval, which didn't disappear when Norma married and left home, or even when her mother emigrated to Australia thirty years ago.

With her own two daughters, Norma has tried — successfully on the whole — to be a more open and less intimidating mother, but at times Karen (27), the younger one, obviously feels the threat of her mother's censure. After her parents split up when she was 13, she felt she couldn't mention her father's name in the house: 'I knew I'd be in for a telling off if I did. I wasn't allowed to visit him or see him, and that hurt me because I'd always been close to him.' Rather than confront her mother's dis-approval, she tends to present a *fait accompli*; on one occasion, she didn't tell her mother she was getting married until after the event, and it was too late to stop her. Although Karen admits that her mother is broad-minded, and doesn't interfere, she shies away from court-ing her displeasure, and by doing so, causes more pain.

Norma says, 'I've often thought about the fact that I haven't known my dad a lot. I was his favourite. The years when I needed him, when I was younger, he wasn't there, so it was all my mum. And she was very strict. She brought us up by the Bible and even now, everything I do I think is this right or is this wrong, would God like it. That's from my mum. I never questioned it, and my daughters haven't now, though I think at times our Karen must think is there a God, look what's happened to me.

'I used to be in awe of my mum, I always seemed that little bit frightened of her. It's because she was really strict, although I know it was for our own good. Even when I was married I felt as if she was still behind me, she could still tell me off.

'She didn't want me to marry my first husband; she said it quite openly, to him as well. At the time I felt it was because she would miss my board — she relied on us to help out and I'm sure that's why she didn't want any of us to get married.

'She used to get really mad with us when we were pregnant, so when you were having another one you used to really dread telling her. She always used to say, "Another baby, you're having another baby?" She had seven herself; she used to say, "I don't want you to make the same mistakes as I've made."

'I was the eldest girl, so everything used to fall on me — take charge of the younger ones, take them out, bath them. That's something I've tried very hard not to do with my two daughters. I've tried to have a relationship with them that they can come and tell me things, that they're not frightened, like I used to be with my mum. I used to think I'll bring mine up different to my mum. At the same time I'm not criticising my mum because it was right for us and she had a difficult job bringing us up on her own.

'When Karen left home to live with her dad I was very upset because she just left me a note to say that she was going. I got up one morning and she'd gone. It upset me a lot, because I thought she was closer to me at that time than she was evidently. It hurt a lot. But you get over it. I told her that she could always come back, that this was her home. There was no bitterness; I think too much of them for there to be bitterness.

'Another thing that Karen did against me was when I had to go into hospital for a big operation. She knew I didn't like this lad she was going with so when I was in hospital she just went and got married to him. After she married him I thought, fair enough, they love each other, that's it. I've never interfered with them — I've tried not

39

to anyway, although I've tried to give them advice some-times. But I've learned from experience that the more I've said don't go with a lad, the more they'd go behind my back and do it. When Karen was 16 she was spending time with a young lad who was parted from his wife and Karen used to sneak down there with a lot more girls. I didn't like it because he still had a wife, so I used to put my foot down.'

Many women feel that their mothers avoid an emotional life with their children by concentrating on the domestic side of the role. Gill felt that her mother had escaped into the 'nursing, caring role' years ago, because she just couldn't handle three children under 5. There simply wasn't enough time or energy for any emotional relationship with them.

Daughters who strive to avoid recreating this emotion-ally barren, but superficially perfect, mother figure, whose children's clothes are always immaculate, and their bodies well-nourished and squeaky clean, are almost bound to run into difficulties. The problem is that mother's voice is always there, inspiring guilt because the bathroom isn't as clean as it might be, the children don't go to bed as early as they should, the man of the house isn't as well looked after as he ought to be.

At 41, Gill still wrestles to understand her 70-year-old mother, who taught her rather emotional little girl to keep a lid on her feelings. The pattern of mother dictating, daughter anxious to please still exists, although Gill is making tentative attempts to change things. She's making much more headway in her conscious efforts to escape her mother's example with her own 5-year-old daughter, Katy, but not without obvious maternal disapproval. Gill makes a point of asking how Katy feels about things, and encouraging her to be aware of her confusing emotions.

Gill also has two teenage sons and another daughter who she gave up for adoption twenty-four years ago. She thinks her mother's lack of awareness of her own feelings was in turn caused by her mother, and she was determined not to affect another generation.

'My mother has always said that she didn't want a daughter; maybe it was because of the unhappiness of her own life. She was alienated from her parents. She was sent to boarding school at the age of 8. When she came home in the holidays the housekeeper looked after her while her parents were abroad. She used to talk to the chickens for company; she must have been very lonely. She's still very institutionalised — you could pack all her things into a trunk.

'I don't think she ever came up to her mother's expectations and I think that's what she's passed on. My grandmother was a matron, but she thought nurses [Gill's mother was a nurse] were the lowest of the low. She thought if you didn't go to university you were the pits. So my mother was brought up in a way that lowered her self-esteem.

'I think if people said I was like my mother I would feel a bit horrified. I'm trying desperately to look for the good things in her so that I can feel good about that part [of me]. I was apprehensive about having a daughter this time, because I thought, am I going to carry on this business, is there something inherent somewhere? But Katy's taught me. I've learned a lot about myself from having Katy, watching her and my reactions to things, much more than my sons.

'I had my second son when I knew that the marriage was over. But it took me years to face up to the fact that marriage didn't go on for ever. I thought that this was your lot. That mentality, of batten down the hatches, soldier on, forget your own happiness, you don't deserve any, all those sillinesses, must have come from my mother.

'When my mother came to stay last Easter, she was awful to Katy, cutting and sarcastic. Both my sons noticed it. I couldn't ring my mother for a month afterwards because I felt so uptight about it. I should have stood up to her when she was here, but I couldn't do it. About three weeks later Katy's eyes glazed over with tears at the meal table when I laughed at her. She said, "Granny was horrible when she was here. She was laughing." I said, "What did it feel like?" And she said, "I felt as if someone had smacked me."

'Katy is very assertive, as children of 5 are. My mother thinks it's terrible; she keeps saying things like, "The boys were never like that." She's saying it in front of Katy, which is not on. Initially I thought perhaps I wasn't the same with the boys, but then I thought it was my mother who was in the wrong.

'There are elements of Katy's behaviour that I actively encourage because I was repressed. I do ask her how she feels about things and she tells me. One day she had a real screaming tantrum sparked off by the teacher saying, "Would you like to say goodbye to your mummy now, Katy? She's going now." When she came home, I asked her about it and she said, "I don't mind it when you go off, but I hate saying goodbye to you, it makes me feel not very nice in my tummy." She described the same kind of tension adults feel.

'I learn a lot from what she says, about her and how I react to her. So when this little child with her shoulders back has got fresh what I'm having to learn in assertiveness classes, I'm not anxious to dampen it down. I encourage her to negotiate, whereas my mother thinks that's a waste of time, you should tell the child and that's the end of it. But life's not like that.

'Katy gets up with me and goes to bed with me. My mother says, "Oh my goodness me, the boys just went to bed and that was it." She has every right to say that, but what she has to realise is that we're all changing, and that change is for the better. The way I brought the boys up is much closer to the way my mother brought me up. She was a smacker, and I've had to restrain myself, because there's that in me too. I suppose I'm objecting to her inability to change with us.

'I don't put on a front with my mother any more, because I found it too much of a strain. I used to get out my tablecloths, and I tried to be really finnicky, and I really hated anybody coming round. In the end I was just slinging mince on the table and my mother would say, "This isn't quite what you used to do," and I'd say, "I'm not that sort of person." The real person is now emerging.

I've tried to link the times when I've been myself to all the other times when I've done what other people expect — the other mothers at the school gate, the people when I was a secretary in the probation office. I look at that, and I think, damn, I'm only just beginning to emerge.'

Diane, a 50-year-old American who was brought up in the USA and who now lives in Scotland, echoes the feelings of many daughters who think that their mothers' dedication to the domestic ideal ruled out any chance of a close relationship. Her mother's lack of interest in her personal appearance is typical of the classic perfect mother figure, who has neither the time nor the inclination for such frivolous matters. To an outsider it expresses a lack of identity outside the anonymous identity of 'mother', which may inspire respect, but very rarely much interest.

'My mother was a difficult woman and I was determined I was never going to be like her. She always looked old, I don't ever remember her looking young or glamorous. Once, when I wanted her to look after one of the girls she said, "I've spent my whole life bringing up children and I'm not going to start looking after my children's children." I was resentful of that and I thought, I will never be like that. I was aghast that my mother had these anti-child feelings and yet we came from this enormous family with children everywhere. I had three sisters, and my father was away in the War. She never lost those feelings of resentment and tried to pass them over to her own daughters.

'It was a non-relationship. There was no role model whatever from my mother. She was a mother who was there. She did all the traditional motherly things — cooking, sewing, etc. — but she was not a mother you could talk to or be close to. She didn't understand her feelings, she didn't explain being a teenager to me, she was impatient when we had boyfriends.

'She didn't tell me about periods, I found out from a girlfriend. I was embarrassed to tell my mother when they started. I remember going to her and saying, "You know that thing you get, well it's happened." And that was it, there was no discussion.

'My own adolescence was hell. I'd never want to live through that period again and I've not wanted that for my daughters. I've wanted them to have a really well-rounded life. You can't protect them from the pain, but I've wanted them to have opportunities like dancing lessons, music lessons, quality education, to have their friends in the house.'

With her younger daughter, Sarah, Diane's efforts have evidently paid off. They have a close, mutually supportive relationship (which they talk about in Chapter 4, The Teenage Years). In fact, in her efforts to be the opposite of her mother as far as looks go, Diane has almost been too successful — Sarah was taken aback when one of her ex-boyfriends started chatting up her mother.

Sally, who is 35 and has a 16-year-old daughter, Polly, and two younger sons, made a conscious decision that she would never be the kind of mother to her children that her mother had been to her — totally domesticated and devoted. Her mother's death at the age of 55 last year brought home to Sally the bitter truth of her mother's life, which she sacrificed to her six children without question. Sally also feels a degree of anger about the way her mother seemed to condone what she describes as her father's mental abuse of his children. In her own marriage she has reacted against the role model of authoritarian husband-submissive wife that her parents presented.

'I've always told Polly and the others that I'm never going to be a mother to them like my mother was to me. There were six of us, but everything ran like clockwork, all our clothes were always ironed and mended. There's no way that I'll be like that for my children.

'After she died we realised we didn't know who she was, the only thing she was was our mother. Apart from that I don't think she really existed. At her funeral this stupid priest said, this woman was a saint, she had all these children and she did so much for other people. Afterwards my sister said to me, that's why she died, because she never did a bloody thing for herself. When birthdays and Christmasses came, we never knew what to give her, yet

we all adored her, and we were always aware that my
father was horrible to her. Looking back on it, she should
have stood up to him, but she was just completely beaten
down.

'I never heard my mother make any demands until she
was dying. Even days before her death, my sister and I
told her she was dying and asked her if she wanted to go
into hospital or stay at home. She said she would go into
hospital, because it would be less trouble for us. We said,
"Look, you've got to do what you want to do." And she
said that she would really rather be at home. It was so
tragic that the only time we could do anything for her was
literally as she died. Two days before she died she said, "I
don't want that sheet, I want a yellow one." We were so
happy because at last there was something she wanted
that we could do. That's just pathetic, that she had to be
dying before she could say what she wanted.

'She always kept out of quarrels. I can remember her
sobbing when my father had me in a corner, but she would
never tell him to stop. I'll never stand by Tom just
because he's my husband, and I'm the woman and I
support him, not even in public. I think that's all so false.
My mother's attitude was, he's your father, you've got to
do what he says. I couldn't understand that, it didn't
make sense.

'I can remember once, during an acupuncture treatment, suddenly feeling this tremendous anger towards my
mother. I went straight home and shut myself in the sitting room and got out my diary and wrote pages and pages
as if I was writing to my mother. I'd never realised it
before, because I thought it was something you can't feel.
And that was real anger towards my mother for letting my
father treat me the way he did.

'I think in our family set up, and in the whole of society,
your mother is your protector, the ultimate barrier
between you and the rest of the world. My mother stood
back and let someone torment me for years and she let
him torment her. As I grew older, I intellectualised it and I
understood she was in no position to do anything, but I

think I suppressed those tremendous feelings of anger. I never talked to her about it, I couldn't see the point. It wouldn't have done me any good and it would only have upset her.

'I think my mother chose to die rather than confront my father and change her life. She had her children, that was the whole meaning of her life, and shortly after the youngest grew up and left home she died.

'On Christmas Eve liver cancer was diagnosed and she died in January. She said, "You'll never forget this Christmas, will you?" In some ways, when she said things like that I felt that somehow she's able to know exactly how we feel about her, because we were all there all the time. There was no doubt about how we felt about her dying. It's brought us all so close. In some ways I'd never seen my mum so happy and contented as that. It almost seemed as if at last my mother had done something that she wanted, that in dying she had taken control of herself and her life.'

4.
THE TEENAGE YEARS

'Maxine was difficult. Once I had the police round for under-age drinking. But I tried to listen to things on the telly and understand it all. Not like my parents did. I want to try and understand, because I want us to be mates.'

Maureen

'People talk about the problems teenagers have, and the emotional upsets they go through, but nobody says anything about the parents. And yet it's as new to them as it is to the children, and it can be just as difficult.'

Gerda

The teenage years are a notoriously difficult time for mothers and daughters alike. In the red corner stands the teenager, suffering moods, depression, spots, and a lethal combination of hopeless inadequacy and unspeakable arrogance. In the blue corner stands mother, anxious about everything from heroin to AIDS (neither of which had raised their ugly heads in her day), and hysterical with worry when her daughter stomps out of the house in the tiniest of mini-skirts and the tightest of T-shirts, but too fearful of the inevitable outburst to voice a word of caution.

Of course, it's not always quite like this. To many daughters of the sixties generation, their own lives seem deadly boring compared to their mothers' thrilling, sexually active, youth. And as ageism creeps out of women's dress, many mothers have a style and youthfulness which their own mothers lacked, and which can prove a bit of a challenge to their young ugly duckling.

47

For some mothers and daughters, adolescence passes with no more than a few mild arguments — many of the women I spoke to said their teenage sons were much more difficult — while for others, it means years when mother and daughter are on opposing sides of a battleground from which they may, or may not, emerge unscathed for life. Often it's a question of gritting the teeth and bearing it, with the motto 'All things must come to an end' engraved on your heart.

For many mothers, their daughter's adolescent years are a time of deep disappointment. For years they've been looking forward to a sisterly friendship, which often cannot begin to develop until their daughters have grown up and grown away — if it develops at all, that is. More than anything, adolescence is a time of learning to let go, to stop thinking about the daughter as a child and see her as an adult, capable of making her own decisions without your help, which is, of course, much easier said than done.

In early adolescence girls aren't old enough to make some decisions, they just think they are, and that's when the battles start. As a mother, the trick is to keep open the channels of communication at all costs — useless advice if those channels were never opened in childhood. You can't expect your daughter to suddenly start telling you the intimate details of her confusing life if you never talked to her as a child.

Gerda, who is 42 and has two daughters on the brink of adulthood, says she was always anxious for them to grow up; she always treated them as 'little adults'. Gerda and her younger daughter Rachel, who is 19, enjoyed what Gerda describes as a growing closeness until a particularly rocky period from 14 onwards, when Rachel was a punk, went around with a 'bad crowd', and generally did everything a mother dreads, including running away from their home in a small Derbyshire village to London. For both mother and daughter it was an unforgettable experience, and a turning point. They have emerged from Rachel's traumatic teenage years with an unbreakable bond. As Gerda explains: 'I always thought, if I ever have children, they must be able to get through to me, and vice versa. But for all your good intentions, they get to be a certain age and it doesn't work. My daughters and I are very close now, especially the younger one, but there were times when I would look at her and there was a stranger sitting there. People talk about the problems teenagers have, and the emotional upsets they go through, but nobody says anything about the parents. And yet it's as new to them as it is to the children, and it can be just as difficult. These days they have parent lines, but they didn't when I was going through those problems with my daughters.

'The older one was difficult from about 12 to 16; with the younger one 14 to 16 were the worst years. It was dreadful — the abusive language, they wouldn't wash, they wouldn't eat, especially the younger one. She got in with a bad crowd and that put a tremendous strain on things, plus the fact that I was going through my second bad marriage, so I was piggy in the middle all the time. My husband was a very old-fashioned man, who believed you're 15 today, you can't go out with boys, you're 16 tomorrow, you can bring one home — very irrational. I was trying to bridge a gap; sometimes I succeeded but at other times it was impossible. It must be bad enough for parents who are stable in their relationship to cope with growing up daughters.

'When I married my second husband, who was the exact opposite of their father, of course the girls rebelled. That situation continued throughout my marriage, with my girls feeling resentful towards me because they felt I was siding with their stepfather.

'Rachel and I formed a bond because we've been through a lot of bad times together; I don't think the bond will ever be broken. I don't see her so much as my daughter as a friend. We had a similar feeling when she was younger, right up until she started going through this teenage stage when she was about 14, where she was rude, she went punk, she had tattooes, she flunked all her O levels, she did anything and everything; she even ran away from home. Up until that moment it was a growing relationship, but that cut it dead for some time because I couldn't understand her. I couldn't get through to her and she couldn't get through to me. I tried the softly softly approach and I tried to be really hard, then I tried the couldn't care less attitude, which wasn't me anyway, and she knew that.'

Rachel, for her part, explains why she ran away, and why she felt the need to rebel: 'I ran away because I hated my dad full stop and although I couldn't see it at the time my mum was always in the middle. One night I'd just had enough so I went. I left a note, and that was it. After the first couple of days I knew mum would be worried, and that was the only reason I came back. My dad said, "What have you come back for?"

'I used to be a bit punkified. Mum and dad went to Tenerife for a fortnight to patch things up and when they got back I'd shaved my hair in a Mohican. Mum went wild. I used to go out in the evening looking all nice, but with bondage boots and black leggings stuffed up my jumper. I used to change back again in the graveyard before I got home.

'I just wanted to stand up and let somebody know I was there, that I was somebody different. I didn't want to be treated like I was at home. I wanted people to notice me; I wanted to stand out. It's hard to explain, looking back on it; in some of the old photos I look really rough. But it made me feel good; because of my clothes I could be anybody I wanted to be. I could be really loud and no one would bother; because of the clothes I wore they expected that. What put me off was when I walked down the road in my bondage boots and my pink Mohican, the old ladies would cross over; that broke my heart, because I really love old people. The crowd I went around with took drugs, but I never did.'

This was what worried Gerda most: 'That's what I used to be afraid of. I knew that I hadn't lost her, but she was estranged from me, and I knew that this crowd had an awful lot of influence over her. I thought, if I lose her altogether, she's going to get in all sorts of bother. But at the same time, we'd already started to build up a relationship before she went wappy, so I hoped it would be strong enough to make her see sense when it came to the crunch.

'Then she ran away and I thought, "That's it; eight out of ten kids get picked up at the station and used as prostitutes." I was so worried. She'd left that morning for school as normal, and I was at work, so I didn't find out till later. When she wasn't home by half past four I thought that's strange, she didn't say she'd be late. By half past five I was beginning to get worried. I could sense that something wasn't quite right. I rang a few of her friends, and then it clicked. I went up to her room and found the note. I rang the police. I couldn't eat, I daren't go to sleep at night in case I didn't hear the phone ring downstairs; I couldn't work; I couldn't do anything. You just imagine the most awful things happening to her. Then she was spotted in London — I thought, Oh no, anywhere but London — then she was seen nearer home and then she rang. I said, "Just come home, I'm sure whatever it was we can sort out." She came home the next day.

'The relief that she was all right was tremendous. Then it was just getting over the trauma. Half the time she'd been sleeping in a barn and she smelled like a pole cat; it was horrendous. That day was a turning point for us. I don't know what she expected when she came home.'

'A real good hiding from my dad,' says Rachel. 'I knew my mum would be mad, but that she'd be overcome with joy at seeing me and forget about giving me a good hiding if I was lucky. I wanted to go home the first day, but I wouldn't because of my dad. When I wrote out my statement at the police station, I couldn't even remember how long I'd been gone for. I couldn't remember the day or the date.'

Rachel's behaviour reminds Gerda of her own childhood: 'It shocked me because what I was witnessing was what I had done as a child. I ran away from my grandmother, who brought me up, five times. I loved her, but I hated the man she had married, and he hated me. It really brought it home to me what my grandmother must have gone through. The guilt feeling was dreadful. I thought, history's repeating itself; you are now being punished for what you did to your grandmother.

'Running away is a horrible thing, because you're so confused; you want to get away from a situation which at the time seems unbearable. The problems Rachel had were so small compared to the problems we've had since, but at the time they must have seemed gigantic to her. The only way she could cope with the situation was to run away. That's how it was with me.'

It's never been easy to prepare a teenage daughter for sex. In some respects, the days when it was a taboo subject must have been a blessed relief to many mothers, if not to their confused daughters. Peggy, who is in her seventies, recalls the misconceptions she had about the subject as a young woman: 'When I went up to university I was very ignorant about sex. I can remember thinking I mustn't let a man hold me too tightly on the dance floor or I might get pregnant.' Ina, who is also in her seventies, says, 'My mother never told me about sex at all. I heard about it in school, but not from the teachers! People would say it and I thought to myself, that's a load of rubbish, but eventually it worked into my mind that that was right. I don't remember mother ever saying anything to me about periods either. When my first period started I didn't know what to say. I don't know how I eventually did tell her what had happened.'

Of course, it's always been the case that girls learn a lot more about periods and sex from their friends or elder sisters than they do from their mothers, and that will probably never change. Many of the daughters I interviewed said that their mothers hadn't told them about sex, though the mothers of the same girls usually claimed that they had!

Menstruation is a different matter; most mothers manage to tell their daughters about it, although many said they felt very embarrassed. They're often prompted by some impending event, like a trip away from home, when their daughters are of an age when their periods could start any time.

Joanne's mother Heather told her about menstruation when she was 9. 'It was when I'd just got back from a holiday abroad, and I had a lot of mosquito bites on my legs. Mum got me up in my room at night time and started telling me about it and showing me a book. She was embarrassed about it and so was I. She told me to read the book, but I didn't want to because I felt funny. I know I was nervous because I was scratching my leg. When she'd finished and I got up to walk out I had all blood down my legs; I thought my period had started, but it was only where I'd been scratching my mosquito bites.'

Joanne took the cue from her mother throughout her teenage years; because, as she says, 'In a way I felt embarrassed about growing up' she didn't tell her mother when she started using tampons, and hid the razor for shaving her legs under the bed. This kind of secrecy will certainly be familiar to more women than not. It seems trivial, but the reason it matters is that embarrassment is infectious, and so the idea that neither menstruation, nor sex, nor women's bodies, are really very nice gets passed on from generation to generation. The trouble is, you can't stop people being embarrassed; you either blush or you don't. What's more, the information, or lack of it, that comes from mother's lips, plus the emotion that is communicated whether she likes it or not, are likely to be more firmly engrained than anything else.

Gill, now 41, got pregnant when she was 16; the baby, Karen, was adopted. She says her mother's explanation of sex was painfully inadequate because it was too clinical: 'I met Karen's father on holiday on a farm in the New Forest. The sexual relationship opened up doors; I felt free. I knew nothing about contraception; I knew how babies were made because my parents had told me in what was like a biology lesson. But that bears no relevance to the feelings you have when you're 15 or 16. A piece of paper with a diagram on it can't describe that.'

Helen, who admits she hasn't refreshed her 16-year-old daughter's memory about sex since she was 11, explains why she would rather her daughter delayed her sex life for the time being at least, even though — or perhaps because — she was sleeping with Claudia's father at the same age. 'If Claudia were sleeping with someone I'd feel a little regret that it was the end of her childhood, because that's going to be the pattern for the rest of her life from then on — sex is going to be a part of any other relationship. And I suppose it is an added complication in a certain way. Having said that it would depend on the man and my immediate reaction would be to worry more about AIDS than pregnancy. I'd be concerned that she was using barrier contraception.'

The current generation of teenage girls faces a quite different set of problems to the problems their mothers faced as teenagers: Gerda's main worries when Rachel ran away centred on sexual disease, prostitution and drugs. AIDS and herpes have forced a revolution in the nation's sexual habits more dramatic than the sexual revolution of the sixties.

Maeve, a lesbian mother of two daughters aged 16 and 18, used to live in a commune in the late sixties and early seventies. She feels a certain sadness that her daughters' future will be blighted by the threat of AIDS. Like many of their peers, her daughters seem to have adopted a much tougher moral line than the previous generation, yet they are totally accepting of their mother's sexual preference.

'When the government first put out all those programmes about AIDS I felt really weepy about it all, thinking of how different my daughters' early sexual experiments would be to what my life had been at 18, 19, 20. The whole idea of having to interview your potential partner as to their previous sex life seemed really awful at first, but then I began to see that a lot of positive things could come out of it, in terms of people being more open with each other, the relationship being much more important. It certainly would seem to put a stop to the kind of jumping into bed with people at parties without even knowing names that people did in the late sixties — but that's probably no bad thing.

'I think my daughters definitely have a stricter moral

line than I did at their age, although it's hard to know because the whole climate of what is acceptable has changed so much. We lived in a commune at one time and the press quite often used to ring up and want to come and film us or interview us and they'd always ask, "Do you have group sex?" and we'd say no and they'd lose interest immediately. You can't imagine that happening now. The girls do seem more squeamish about the idea of sex than I was at that age, but then it's really hard to remember.

'It's fairly recent that I came out openly. I was afraid of losing custody of the children because various friends of mine had. Although they drive me bonkers as teenagers I couldn't have coped with them being sent off into care or to live with in-laws — it's just unthinkable. I've always been bisexual. I'd slept with my women friends for years. I remember discussing the first relationship that I'd think of as a lesbian relationship, with another woman who identified as lesbian, with my older daughter. She shrugged her shoulders and said, "You just love people, it doesn't matter what sex they are."

'I don't know whether or not my daughters go out with boys — that's one big area that may be a secret, I don't know. They don't seem to show a great deal of interest in relationships at the moment. They sometimes tease me and say, "You wish we were having relationships, you wish we were wild like you were in the sixties." Maybe they're biding their time until they leave home. They've got this whole analysis about why hippy parents have ultra-straight kids. They think they're reacting to me, by being really ordinary and straight. We don't have rows about them staying out late. If anything it's the other way round — if I come home late they look at their watches and say where have you been?'

When Maeve was a teenager, she suffered from anorexia, another, more insidious, epidemic affecting thousands of teenage girls every year. 'I started fasting when I was about 14. I went on to have bulimia in my mid-twenties, during the last couple of years of my marriage. It got really bad when I was first on my own with the kids.

Then I managed to get some help. In therapy we used trance and quite often I'd revisit chunks of childhood I'd completely forgotten about and often there were family conflicts going on around meals. I really needed to sit back and objectively see the ridiculousness of it all, of the stupid, fanatical things they thought were important about manners and eating and behaviour. I just needed to be myself, not this mannerly, manicured person that they were trying to produce. That's what a lot of the conflict was about I think.

'I know from what I've read since that anorexia seems to be a lot to do with the person needing to have control over some part of their life and I didn't feel I had much control over my life at all. That's the sort of theory that holds water for me. I felt intruded upon by both my parents for much of my life. I didn't really have a sense of myself as separate from them; I felt terribly dutiful towards both of them a lot of the time. And I seem to have reproduced that — what is quite a cruel relationship — in my long-term relationships with men.'

Anorexia is generally regarded as a disease affecting white, middle-class girls: Chanell, who started to suffer from anorexia when she was 12, and battled with the disease throughout her teenage years (she is now 19), is one of many exceptions. She blames her illness, rightly or wrongly, on her mother, who came to England from Pakistan soon after she was married, and on the culture clash which has driven a wedge between them. But at the same time, she struggles to understand her mother, who she now visits only rarely. At the moment Chanell's over-riding feeling for her mother is blame, though at one point she did say, half-jokingly, that in ten years' time they might be the best of friends.

'I started to stop eating straight after my first period, when I was 12. Once a Muslim girl starts menstruation, she's married off. She's seen as ready to be that baby machine, to be that cooker and carer and cleaner.

'I think my mother tried to inflict a lot of that on us, trying to put us in arranged marriages and so on, because

that's what happened to her at 16. She was a very intelli-
gent woman and unfortunately she ended up in an
arranged marriage. I think that's all she saw that there
was to life. She finds it very difficult to love, because of her
own past. She's one hell of a woman, but I've got very little
respect for her. There's very little emotion between me
and her and between the rest of her daughters and her. We
have very little contact with her; I would say we're
estranged from her, although deep down, I think I love
her.

'I was rushed into hospital after I took an overdose
when I was 13. Being in hospital was probably one of the
most distressing experiences I've had, but it was the only
option for me. There was a girl in the same ward who also
had anorexia — we supported each other a great deal, and
her mother supported me too.

'My sister had to tell my parents I was in hospital. My
mother and father were very concerned that it wasn't the
done thing. My mother only visited me three times: at the
time I didn't think about it much, but now I look back and
I think what a shitty thing to do. That's the way she coped
with it.

'When I came out of hospital I went back to school, then
I went back into hospital when I was 16. Then I moved out
and went to live with my brother and I made a very good
recovery. I haven't slipped back into anorexia since leaving my mother's home. It must be really awful for her to
have to live with that.

'I never tackled therapy until I left home. Everything in
therapy comes back to the mother-daughter relationship
and the culture clash. My therapist is an Indian woman,
which helps. There were so many things my mother did, so
many reactions she had that I accepted as normal; being
in full-time therapy you discuss these small things and
you didn't realise at the time what an impact they had on
you.

'We were dominated by religion — it was forced down
our throats. When I was 9 my mother lost a daughter who
was 4 weeks old. Soon after that she started pumping

religion into us, making us read the Koran for two hours every night. She's been an unhealthy fanatic for ten years now; she's got no interests outside the home except religion. I've rejected all that. These days I'm trying to open my eyes to the culture more than the religion. I haven't got any Indian clothes; when I left my mother I left all that behind, but now I'm getting interested in Indian sewing and fabrics. I look at my mother now and think she's a victim of her own culture. I really do pity her because she's had a very distressing life.

'I daren't ask her about contraception. We never discussed anything like that. I didn't really know what periods were; I found out about them in the school playground. I remember the day I started my period. Her reaction was "Not another one".

'Within the culture and within the family, food was very important. Obviously you've got fasting, then you have the big celebrations of food, and you always bless food before you eat.

'It would be a lie for me to say I don't worry about food every day, because I do. I do laxative abuse still, and I exercise fanatically. But it's not an obsession because I know I have to keep myself busy, it's the only way I'm going to survive.

'I've seen my mother once or twice this year. If we speak on the phone we're polite to each other under duress. When I see her we still argue about marriage; she used to want us to marry an Asian Muslim, but now anyone will do. She thinks sex before marriage is an absolute sin. It's an absolute horror to my mother that my sister has a baby outside marriage.

'I don't enter into relationships with men if I can avoid it. A sexual relationship is too difficult for me to deal with even now, because of my body, because I'm so screwed up about it.

'My mother used to be very slim and very beautiful; now she's a mess. She's put her body through a lot — seven children and a miscarriage and a hysterectomy. She's aware that she's fat now, but at 50 she's still very young-looking.

'My mother also has a hard time within the community, because she's the only one who's got daughters as old as this who aren't married, so she's under pressure from her friends as well.

'As sisters we had support from each other to rebel. We all admit we might have made pigs' ears of our own lives, but we've got a hell of a lot of years to go to rectify it.

'I'd love my mother to be someone else for a day, and to actually tell me how she felt about me. It makes me angry that she won't talk about anything dreadful that's happened in the family. I'd like to have a distant relationship with my mother. We'll probably be best friends in a couple of years. I'd do a lot of things different with my daughters — one thing I wouldn't do is give them beautiful names because that really screws you up.'

At the opposite extreme of Chanell's virtual estrangement from her mother is an ideal of the relationship, in which mother and teenage daughter are like friends, only better, swapping fashion notes and beauty tips, keeping no secrets, telling no lies. . . . It's an ideal which rarely exists, but which haunts many mothers, making them feel inadequate and wondering where they went wrong.

Sally is acutely conscious that her relationship with her 16-year-old daughter, Polly, falls short of the ideal she has in her mind. It's surely no coincidence that Sally experienced the same feeling of disappointment in her relationship with her own mother, who died recently. Sally blames her inability to make contact with her daughter on the fact that she had no satisfactory role model of a mother-daughter relationship to base it on. Her teenage years were characterised by deception and lies, to get around the strict rules her father laid down and her mother upheld.

In contrast, she makes few rules: 'I place virtually no restrictions on Polly. The restrictions I place on her are those I feel have to be there because there's five of us living in the house together. I don't try to control her personality. I can't see that there would be any rules at all. She's never been out on a date, she's never stayed out late at night. I suppose if she were doing things like that I would want to know where she was so I wouldn't worry. On several occasions I've explained to her that any woman with any sense doesn't walk down dark alleyways by herself, and that there are certain things that you don't do if you're a woman.

'My mother was incredibly unphysical. I have nothing to base my relationship with Polly on, nothing at all. It's like a void. My sisters feel the same. My mother never touched me at all. The only time I can remember touching her was when she was dead. She wouldn't let me touch her when she was alive; it was as if there was a wall.

'I feel I know exactly how Polly is feeling, exactly what she's going through, and yet I cannot comfort her or do anything about it. With Henry [Sally's 12-year-old son] I think, something's going on in his life and he's unhappy, but I can't relate to it at all. Yet somehow I'm more able to comfort him, whereas with Polly I'm absolutely sure that what she feels about something or somebody is precisely how I used to feel and yet I can't do anything about it. The first time she fell in love I really wanted to talk to her about it, because I know how she felt. I can remember the first person I fell in love with and what it was like. And I know how she feels in her relationships with the girls at school and yet I've never talked to her about it. I can't because it doesn't arise out of our conversation.

'I remember wanting to talk to my mother and I suppose I've idealised a relationship which doesn't ever really exist, a sort of pally relationship between a mother and daughter. I know that's what I always wanted with my mother, and so I think I should be able to have it with Polly, and I haven't. But does it exist? I don't know.

'She talks to Tom, her stepdad, who came to live with us when she was 2, more than she does to me; they're really good friends. I just don't talk to her. It sounds awful, but I feel as if I don't have any relationship with her. Certainly not that I would like, anyway.

'I want her to be really open with me and tell me things and she doesn't and if she did it would be forced, not real.

It's very sad, I really regret it. Perhaps I was too young when I had her, I don't know. And I feel guilty that I took her away from her father, but I don't talk to her about it. Once I said to her, if you want to know anything about it, ask me, because I don't mind talking about it. I'll tell you anything you want to know. I don't want you to spend all your life wondering about something, because I always wondered about things and if I asked my parents they wouldn't tell me. So I said that to her and it just seemed to embarrass her. Yet she's very open and chatty with other people.'

For Diane and her daughter, Sarah, an almost ideal relationship has existed since the beginning of Sarah's teenage years; she is now 18. The circumstances of their lives are far from ideal, however; the bond between them was sealed by the temporary breakdown of Diane's marriage two years ago. Since Sarah, the youngest of three daughters, was born Diane has felt a particular closeness to her. This grew with the development of shared interests, like acting and going to the theatre and ballet, interests which Sarah's sister, a sporty, outdoorsy type, did not share. Like any friendship, a close relationship between mother and daughter thrives on common ground which provides a basis for communication. Whether these shared interests develop, however, seems to be a matter of luck — mothers who try too hard to point their daughter towards a particular passion of their own are as often as not met with a healthy reaction in a quite different direction!

Diane and Sarah developed a ritual which became the focus of their relationship throughout Sarah's teenage years. Diane explains: 'When she was about 12, Sarah started drinking tea and I always waited until she came home from school to have my own tea — her older sister doesn't like tea or coffee and she didn't take part in this. It became a little ritual that we had and it still exists. We always wait for each other to have tea. If there's ever an occasion when we don't have tea together she gets quite annoyed, and vice versa. A few years ago I started collecting china cups and plates for Sarah, and when she leaves home I'll give her them as a memory of mother and daughter having tea.'

Yet Diane and Sarah's relationship, though undoubtedly very close, is not without its complications, which centre on looks. Diane is a very stylish, young-looking 50-year-old; she and Sarah shop in the same places. Diane has strong views on the way Sarah dresses — like so many mothers, she feels her daughter could make a lot more of herself.

'I can remember having squabbles when she was younger and wanted to wear very high heels with very tight jeans, which didn't suit her. Then I really put my foot down and she was very disappointed.

'Then Sarah became very self-conscious about her figure; she has quite a large bust. I think she's slowly getting over this and accepting her body for what it is. But she went through a spell of trying to hide it by wearing big, thick, long jumpers, and she wore black a lot, she didn't want to wear anything that would reveal herself at all. In the last year she's been getting over this. Now she wears quite revealing, strappy dresses.

'Meanwhile I'm quite envious of Sarah's figure, certainly the bust — I would love to have a terrific figure and thick wavy hair like her. When she was little I marvelled at the fact that this was my daughter — I don't have hair like that.

'Sarah said to me quite recently, "You don't know how difficult it is to have a mother who is attractive to her own boyfriends." It brought me up short. I think it came about because a boy who called round to see her asked if I was Sarah's sister. When she told me this I thought it was terribly funny and then, when I was at Sarah's prize day I went over to speak to a boy who had been in a play with Sarah. He is quite a ladies' man and he was a bit flirtatious and he asked Sarah about me later on and made some approving remarks. Again, I thought it was funny. It was later that she made the remark and I thought, I'm going to have to watch this, I didn't know she had these feelings.

'I don't think she's jealous of me, I just think it's something that's been bubbling under the surface for a long time, that she's always been conscious of my looks. And yet it never surfaced, it was never discussed. We did go shopping a lot together, we still do, we're both very style-conscious. I don't feel jealous of her, though sometimes I wish I could step back in time and have the opportunities she is having now.'

Sarah recalls the same incident: 'The first boy I ever went out with met my mum for the first time four weeks ago and he was in love with her. He didn't stop talking about her for about two weeks. He thought she was great. I was pleased. I like it when people think my mum's nice, because I think she's really nice. She's pretty easy to get on with because she's quite young-acting. I think my friends are quite surprised when they see her, because she wears trendy clothes.

'I don't tell mum everything, but then I don't have any big secrets. I've got a diary and if she read it I'd murder her. I think she understands me quite well; we're very similar. I'm not a rebellious teenager. I'm not a very complicated person.

'We talk about things you might discuss with a friend — teen talk. We'll discuss my dad. She expects me to have lots of answers about my dad which gets a bit difficult since I never do. So these conversations tend to go round in circles. Some of my friends might not understand the situations I've been through — mum does.'

Sarah and Diane are lucky. Few mothers and daughters have such a close relationship until later in life. When the daughter leaves home it gives both sides a vital breathing space during which, with any luck, they come to see the other in a new light: the daughter as an adult, and the mother as an individual with an existence outside the family.

5.
TEENAGE PREGNANCY

'I just said, a baby is coming and it could be any day. My poor mother, she must have been shocked. I can remember just sitting at the table while she went into a flat spin. I felt cold, bereft of any feeling. It's only now, as an adult, that I can think how awful it was for my mother.'

Gill

'I didn't realise that they were sleeping together. I suppose in a way I thought it was partly my fault; it's not really logical, but I did feel I should have realised the temptation was there.'

Ann

'Mum . . . I think I might be pregnant. . . .' Those are words which any mother of teenage daughters dreads. An unwanted teenage pregnancy doesn't just signal the death knell of a mother's long-cherished hopes for her daughter — a good education, a career, the chance to see a bit of life — it also means that the responsibilities of motherhood which the mother knows all too well, but the daughter is blissfully ignorant about, are brought forward. It's significant that women who have had babies when they were teenagers themselves rarely want their daughters to follow in their footsteps.

Peggy, whose daughter Helen had her first baby 16 years ago, at the age of 17, speaks for many mothers in her position when she says, 'My main feeling was the waste, that whatever happens you can't go back. If the baby's adopted or if you marry or whatever, the baby has come and it makes a difference. You can't go back to what you were before. You've got to be marked by it in some way.'

These days, there may be more options open to the pregnant teenager — adoption, abortion or keeping the baby with or without marriage. And thankfully attitudes towards unmarried mothers have softened in the past twenty years. But it doesn't make the decision any easier.

Eighteen-year-old Maxine and her mother Maureen arrived at the decision that Maxine should have an abortion together. Having terminated two pregnancies herself, Maureen was able to sympathise with the way her daughter felt. She encouraged Maxine to have an abortion because she felt it would stop her making the mistakes she feels she's made in life. Maxine's 17-year-old brother Mitchell, who is severely brain damaged after a bout of meningitis at 3 months, was also an influential factor.

Maureen voices a dilemma which many mothers feel about the Pill. She didn't want to encourage Maxine to take it on health grounds, and recent reports linking the Pill with breast cancer have proved that her fears were well founded. Yet she realises it's unreasonable to expect her daughter to be celibate. Ann, whose daughter Christine decided to keep her baby, was forced to come to the reluctant conclusion that the Pill is the only sure way of avoiding a second unwanted pregnancy in the family; she's made sure both her daughters are now taking it.

Maxine says, 'I wasn't bothered about how mum would react because I knew she would be all right. I just said I've done half of a pregnancy test and it's positive and we sat doing the other half together. Some days I wanted to keep the baby, some days I didn't.'

Maureen says, 'I'm not a mother living in the dark ages. Maxine's friend said to me I wouldn't dare tell my mum if I was pregnant, she'd kill me. I didn't dare tell my mum and dad that I was pregnant, I was frightened to death. I didn't want Maxine to go through that, I didn't want her to have that kind of pressure.

'The thing is, Maxine has helped me look after Mitchell. She's not gone out at nights when she's wanted to, and things like that. She's never had a proper job. I didn't want her saddled down with a baby. I think she needs to get a bit of life behind her first. I never did, you see. I was 22 and pregnant when I got married, and I knew nothing at all about life. I don't want her to make that mistake.

'When the second half of the pregnancy test was positive, I don't think she believed it. I had to do all the running about for her. I rang and made the doctor's appointment, I had to drag her out of bed to take her, and she wouldn't even touch the water sample!

'I've never wanted Maxine to go on the Pill. I was only on it for four years myself and I didn't like the idea of it at all, abusing her body and all the rest of it. I think it's a feather in her cap that she's only been having sex recently. She's been going out with her boyfriend for five years and she didn't give in to him until Christmas, and then she fell bloody pregnant.'

When Gill got pregnant at the age of 16, twenty-four years ago, the only option open to her was adoption — at least, that's what the social workers said. Certainly she was too late for an abortion — she didn't tell any adults she was pregnant until four days before her daughter's birth, and somehow her mother managed to ignore her expanding girth. Although Gill admits she wasn't capable of bringing up a child on her own, her memories of the terrible pain of giving up her daughter remain as powerful and distressing today as they ever were.

'Missing periods didn't make me aware of anything. Finally I decided I had to tell someone what I'd done because it was weighing heavy. So I told my best friend, who was one of the tarty girls in the class, and she was shocked rigid. She shouted at me like a parent would, "How could you?" It was when the baby started moving that I realised that I was pregnant.

'I stayed at school for the whole time. The year before last the social worker told me my mother would have known I was pregnant, but she denied it. About four days before Karen was born I went to my GP because my friend was beside herself with worry, and I realised I needed help. I told my mother I was going because of my spots. The baby was kicking, and I used to cuddle the bump at night. I used to think, someone will show me the way.

'The doctor was lovely, and he said you really must go home and tell your parents. I went home and just told them. I wasn't frightened, I just said a baby is coming and it could be any day. My poor mother, she must have been shocked. I can remember just sitting at the table while she went into a flat spin. I felt cold, bereft of any feeling. It's only now, as an adult, that I can think how awful it was for my mother. I've never spoken to her about that day. I really must share it with her before she dies, but I haven't been able to yet.

'There was a quiet atmosphere in the house. Four days later I felt a twinge and my father took me to the hospital, said goodbye and I didn't see him. He came in once when he had to be there while I signed some paper. My mother didn't come at all. I stayed there a week, then I went off into a world unknown with strangers — the mother and baby home in Walton-on-Thames. We had a strict regime to follow, and to all intents and purposes you were the mother. I didn't know what was to come. It was just unreal. The girls all clung tightly to each other. It was a very sad time for all of us. Some of the other girls could scream and shout, but I couldn't.

'I was very protective of the baby's father. The people at the home had no understanding of the feelings I'd had at that time and I didn't want them to spoil it. It was such an idyllic time for me. They made everything dirty and it wasn't like that.

'The social workers felt that because I was educated, there was no question about what I should do. I allowed myself to be put along the road to adoption, because it would be best for the child, because they said I couldn't ruin her chances. And I was too young, there was no way I was capable.

'The day people came to view — it was rather like a shop — you knew could be the final day, so you made use of every day you had with the baby. It was really like the first months that you spend with a lover. I'd also developed this fantasy that it wasn't going to happen.

'The day Karen was adopted I was devastated. I kept thinking it's not going to happen. When the time came, and she was nicely dressed, and they locked the door, the feeling was like something being cut out of my stomach. I can remember thinking, they won't like her; it will be all right, and it will be OK for another day. When I was young I'd seen a cow screaming when its two calves were taken. I remember this horrendous noise coming from its stomach. I couldn't make the sound, but this vision came back to me with the pain I had in my stomach.

'Then there was nothing; just complete utter flat depression. They took me home, and I felt that I didn't belong anywhere, that there was nowhere for me now. I tried to cry and my parents' reaction was rather as if I'd cut my knee — forget about it now, up you get. The emotion is all still there; it always will be.' Twenty years later, Karen made contact with Gill. In Chapter 8, Gill and Karen discuss the effect of the long separation on the bond between them.

Gill was envious of the girls at the mother and baby home who changed their minds and were able to keep their babies, thanks to their mothers' support. Gill says of her own parents, who were on the verge of divorce at the time, 'They couldn't look after me, let alone someone I'd produced.'

Many teenage mothers rely heavily on their mother's support without realising what it means to her — usually a postponement of the freedom she's anticipating once her own children have flown the coop. Leaving home was quite an eye-opener to Karen S., whose 11-year-old daughter Donna was born when she was 16. 'I had it easy when Donna and I were living with my mum. She used to look after her. She used to say, "Come on, you go out. I'll have Donna." She was ever so good. Donna is still close to her now, she goes down to her nana's nearly every night and she'll come up the next morning to school. It was lonely when I first got the council house. My mum and I still went to bingo together, and I went home often, but it was a big change, it just being me and Donna.'

Christine's daughter, Ashleigh, is 2, and they live with Christine's mother, Ann, who looks after Ashleigh while her daughter is at college. Ann could be forgiven for feeling hard done by, although the thought doesn't cross her mind: her two teenage sons and Christine's twin also live at home, her husband works overseas, and Ashleigh's arrival postponed Ann's long-cherished plan to go to university.

Christine was 15 and still at school when she got pregnant. Ann remembers how she first found out: 'Christine didn't tell me when she found out she was pregnant. She and Stuart [Christine's boyfriend] ran away to his aunt's in the north of England. It was actually his sister that told me. Christine hadn't said anything to her twin, which I thought was really strange. I could see she wouldn't want to tell me, although I don't know what she thought I would do.

'I came home to find the house empty. When Christine didn't come back at night I phoned up to Stuart's house and eventually his sister told me Christine was pregnant. It was all terribly dramatic. By that time I had realised it had to be something like that or they wouldn't have gone off, so I wasn't that surprised.

'Christine didn't want to have an abortion, and also by the time we found out it was almost too late — it was approaching the sixteenth week — so the doctor wasn't too keen, but Christine didn't want one anyway. I wouldn't have been upset if she had wanted an abortion because she was so young, although I don't like the idea. I don't disapprove of abortion as such, but I think when it's someone who's directly involved with you it's different. I know how I would feel — I don't think I could have had an abortion. Christine certainly didn't consider adoption; that was definitely out.

'She told me they would get married if I wanted them to. All this was going on while my husband was abroad so I had to phone him and tell him what had happened. It was all very difficult. I didn't want them to get married because at that point I wasn't sure how the situation would develop.

'Christine went back to school to sit all her O level exams when she was pregnant, which I don't think I could have done. But Christine didn't seem bothered about what other people would think or say. They have a very different attitude. I don't know whether it's everybody's children or just some people's children, but they don't seem to think that there's anything morally wrong about jumping into bed. I do, but I suppose that's my generation. I don't think anybody should have intercourse until they're physically and mentally capable of looking after a child.

'As teenagers the twins had the odd moment of nobody loves me, but not as bad as the boys at all. They were much worse. The girls are much more conventional; they don't question what I say. And they're quite reserved, you never know what they're thinking. I sometimes think we should discuss things more, but it's very difficult to get them to talk; they're not chatty girls. But then I'm not very talkative; I think Scottish people tend to be very reserved.

'Christine started going out with Ashleigh's father when she was 14. I wasn't sure if it was a good thing; it's difficult to know what to do. She and Ishbel just spent all their time with these boys. I felt they should be going around in a crowd, although it did make life easier because they didn't want to stay out late. I wasn't interested in boyfriends when I was 16 or 17. I was much more interested in hillwalking and cycling. I was 18 when I met my husband, but I had had other boyfriends. And I'd gone to dances and had good fun.

'Obviously I mentioned contraception in passing, but it's not something I put a lot of emphasis on — perhaps I should have done. And I disapprove of the Pill on health grounds; I don't feel it's good to be on it for too long. I told the girls about various different forms of contraception fairly early on and they knew I disapproved of the Pill, which I think may have been a mistake. If Christine had said she wanted to go on the Pill, I wouldn't have stopped her, but I wasn't going to say you've got a boyfriend now, you'd better go on the Pill.

'I didn't know that Christine and Stuart were sleeping together because they weren't doing it here. They were going to Stuart's house at lunchtime which I didn't realise. I don't know what I could have done about it anyway. You can't follow them around, you just have to hope they'll be sensible. Obviously they weren't. I suppose in a way I thought it was partly my fault; it's not really logical, but I did feel I should have realised the temptation was there.

'Christine is on the Pill now, so is Ishbel. I don't know if Ishbel sleeps with her boyfriend, they certainly don't do it here. When Christine got pregnant, I told Ishbel, if you want to go on the Pill you're to say and eventually she did. I don't entirely approve, but I'm not prepared to go through all this carry-on again.

'Christine didn't appear to be worried about what the baby would do to her life. I was. She and Stuart seem to be quite happy to stay at home and not do very much. Even before the baby appeared they didn't go to discos or anything. They're only interested in Ashleigh and nothing else. But it does seem a very dull and unexciting way to live.

'It was me who suggested that I could look after the baby. I couldn't really see any other way around it unless Christine gave up school and I didn't want that. She went back after the baby was born and took Highers [the Scottish equivalent of A levels], then on to college.

'I was slightly dreading having to look after a baby again, but actually I enjoyed it more than I expected to. In a way it's like having a child of your own again, but you're much more relaxed about it. I don't treat her exactly as I would have treated my own; I wasn't so casual. And when the twins were little I was too busy with housework to enjoy them, whereas now there are plenty of adults around to lend a hand.

'I was toying with the idea of going to university when Ashleigh came along. I regret leaving school in the fifth year, but my parents felt they couldn't afford to have me stay at school. I went to night school and did Higher Spanish, and I coped with it. You begin to think your

71

mind has gone — you do all these children's things and your mind doesn't do anything at all.

'I talked to Christine about my experiences of birth, and I also told her that she would probably be quite different. I don't think I could have stayed with her during the labour, and I think she preferred to have Stuart rather than me. I was pleased the baby was a girl although I'm not sure why, perhaps because I thought it would be easier than a boy. Having a baby around again called to mind things that I had completely forgotten.

'Sometimes if Ashleigh cries I tend to get up and see what it is. I think Christine feels that she should be coping with it and I shouldn't interfere; I try not to. If Christine's around I try to stand back and let her take over. Ashleigh stays up quite late — she's up till 10.30 sometimes, which is quite difficult to cope with. I feel the evenings should be free, that she should be away in her bed by 8. Occasionally we get cross with each other, but not very often. We've coped, and actually it all goes along quite nicely at the moment.'

Christine agrees: 'When mum offered to look after the baby it was the perfect answer to everything. I was never worried that mum would take over because Ashleigh's more attached to me I think. She realises that I'm mum and I'm the boss.

'I knew I was pregnant, but it didn't really sink in until it was too late to do anything about it — it was a very slow reaction. I tried to think I wasn't really. I did think about adoption or an abortion but I immediately thought no, definitely not. At first I would have liked to have got married straight away, but now it's quite good the way it is. There's no need to get married and we couldn't afford it anyway.

'I wasn't really all that worried about my parents finding out I was pregnant because I knew that mum wouldn't kick me out of the house or anything. But I was glad I didn't have to tell her in the end. I was coming round to the idea that I'd have to tell Ishbel and Ishbel would have to tell mum. I think mum was more hurt than Ishbel that I'd told Stuart's sister first.

'I think I'm a born housewife. I'd rather not have a job, but again it's the money thing. I'd like to look after Ashleigh all the time. But it was a real shock having to look after a baby. I didn't realise quite how much work there was until she was there. Once you've had one child you think, never again. It's getting used to the fact that here's this baby and you've got to think about her all the time — if you're planning anything you have to think, "This is what I'll have to do with Ashleigh," it's a constant thing at the back of your mind.

'I think having Ashleigh made me understand mum better. If you've had children you understand all the hassles you have to go through bringing them up. You're not one person any more, you're two people.

'At school my close friends were good about me being pregnant. One or two people who I didn't really know said nasty things but Ishbel and another friend put them in their place. Somebody said I'd had Ashleigh after a one-night stand which just wasn't true.

'I didn't tell many people at college that I had a baby. I thought, if it comes up in conversation, then fair enough, but it never really came up. They didn't find out until I took Ashleigh to a college reunion. I was surprised that they weren't surprised, that there wasn't shock on their faces when I turned up with this baby.

'I suppose because there won't be such a wide age gap between me and Ashleigh when she's a teenager we might understand each other a bit better than mum and I — she was 25 when she had us, there's a big difference. We've got quite different taste in clothes and things.

'I do have regrets sometimes. I think I could maybe have gone to art school and had other relationships and so on, but it's just one of those things. I really couldn't do without Ashleigh now. I'm a bit envious of Ishbel because she can go out and meet other people and other boys. I'm happy with Stuart, but I would quite like to have had one or two more relationships. I'm sometimes quite envious that Ishbel can come and go as she pleases. I don't think I'll ever go to art school now, though I might take up art as a hobby. Having said that, mum did her Spanish Higher. But at the moment I'm happy the way it is.'

Ann's mother, Ina, who is in her seventies, views the situation with the objectivity which is the privilege of grandmotherhood: 'When I found out Christine was pregnant I was annoyed for Christine's sake. I really wasn't surprised. I don't know why but it was in my mind before it happened. I was sad for Christine because it makes an awful difference to your life, at that age especially. I felt it was a bit unfair on Ann, especially with Charlie being away, she had it all on her back, but she coped so well that I didn't feel sorry for her. She said that at her age it could have been her baby and I think she tried to look at it from that point of view. I was so surprised at Christine because nowadays girls are all so knowledgeable and there are so many contraceptives. Contraceptives was probably a word I had never heard at that age. You think it's never going to happen to you. But it has.'

Helen, who is now in her mid-thirties, got pregnant when she was 17, after leaving school to work abroad. Like Ann, Helen's mother, Peggy, initially wondered where she had gone wrong, but seventeen years on she thinks differently:

'When Helen left school, I hoped she would get it out of her system. I've often thought about it, and I think I felt very disappointed when she was obviously clever that she wasn't staying at school. I felt she had a lot of potential and it was silly to fritter it away. But she presented us with a *fait accompli*; she had made all the arrangements and got all the money and everything and just went off. We found out afterwards she'd even been to family planning too and I was rather glad about that.

'Of course you always go back over things and think were we expecting too much, did we not give her the sort of life she wanted? You can't help keeping going over it and asking Why, why, why? Nowadays I think it doesn't make much difference what you do. You do your best and hope it will come out right in the end. I suppose to some extent in Helen's case it has, but a lot of people have been hurt in the process.

'Helen wrote to me about visiting some part of Italy. There was a page or two about this and then a break, and it said, "Well, I suppose I may as well tell you I'm pregnant." Just like that. So I went out to see her. It was made very difficult because if there had been any question of the baby being adopted, the baby's Italian grandparents would have adopted it. Which made it an impossible situation, unless Helen had turned her back on Italy. But she would always have known that there was this baby that belonged to her and Lucio.

'My initial reaction was how was I going to stand up to my husband's anger and pain. He started off saying the chap should be horsewhipped — it's amazing the cliches people come out with. I said well the important thing is to think what's the best thing for the baby, not what's best for Helen or for Lucio. I really felt that if it had happened in this country that to have persuaded her to have it adopted would have been the best. Then she could have got on with her life. But in the circumstances this wasn't possible.

'I was rather sorry that they got married, but Helen seemed to see it as the only thing to do. It was difficult to know what to do — we talked and talked. I was staying with friends in Rome and I can remember Helen coming and staying the night; we stayed awake all night, alternately weeping and talking.

'Seventeen years ago the attitudes to unmarried mothers were rather less kind. I can remember visiting a maternity ward myself and there was a woman with an illegitimate child and the nurses and visitors would look at her and I didn't know if Helen could take all that. I myself wasn't worried about what people might think. I would have been quite happy for her not to marry, or to wait until after the baby was born.'

Helen's reaction was much more optimistic than her mother's, largely because she had no idea what she was letting herself in for. After much soul-searching she married the baby's Italian father. Eight years later they separated, and she was forced to leave both her daughter, and her son, who is a year younger, with their father.

'When I first found out I was pregnant, I was quite pleased. I suppose I wanted to have a baby — I don't know why. I found the idea of having somebody else to look after and loving me quite exciting. I was terribly young and totally unrealistic about it. I don't think at that age you realise the responsibilities.

'I can't remember how I told my mother; I think I must have written. I think it was my father who was going on about horsewhipping and my sister turned round and said what sort of way is that for a Christian to behave and put things in perspective. My mother and father came to Rome to meet Lucio, for all they knew he could have been a real old gigolo. They all seemed to get on quite well, though it must have been terribly difficult.

'When I came back to England in July I was still very uncertain about whether to get married or to have the baby adopted or cope on my own. There weren't as many unmarried mothers then as there are now. But in the end we got married; it doesn't sound very passionate, does it? I don't think it was. The marriage lasted quite well for several years, but I was terribly young and it didn't help him being older, and already very moulded character-wise, whereas I wasn't. I think you change an awful lot up to about 25. I think I outgrew him in the end; he hadn't changed at all and I had.

'When Claudia was born I didn't think, "Here is a creature for whom I will be responsible all her adult life." I think I was terribly simple, that sort of feeling never came sweeping in on me. I was just too young really. I felt it more with the second set of children than with the first set. (Helen has two sons by her second marriage; the eldest was born when Claudia was 11.)

'I went to live in Italy when Claudia was 6 months old. I was very excited about it. Of course it was difficult, but it was more difficult when I came home and then had to go back to Italy. I missed my family and English customs like orderly queues. In some ways it was very helpful because it made me far more assertive than I would be if I had just lived in England.

'My mother-in-law was domineering and rather interfering. When I bought my wedding ring, it was she who took me, not my fiancé. We wouldn't come to blows over the children's upbringing, but it was very awkward at times. She never had a daughter, and I don't know if it was because Claudia was the first grandchild or because she was a girl, but she used to have Claudia to stay every Sunday, and sometimes she would stay the night. So she and Claudia were very close. It probably didn't do my relationship with Claudia any good. I suppose if I'd really minded, I wouldn't have let Claudia go. It was nice to have peace and quiet by the end of the week, but on the other hand it meant that we were never that close as a family. It probably made me more distant from Claudia than I would otherwise have been. I always had Gianni to compensate, and as I said before I'd always wanted a boy more than a girl, and Gianni was always very affectionate, as little boys are.

'In the early years I didn't feel I was missing out. If you're living in another culture, there's so much of that to adapt to that you haven't got the same time to miss out on things as perhaps you would if you're living in your own country. It's only later when things become more everyday that you think. ... Yet I don't think I've ever regretted anything because I think that's a waste of time. If I ever felt I was missing out on things I'd think well, I'll have time for them when the kids are older. Not going to university was the one regret of my life and I did that. And I suppose I did have two or three years of delayed youth when I came over here and they were still in Italy, but all it is really is freedom to go out and enjoy yourself.

'Having children young you do have more energy, and I did have more patience then. And of course, you're closer to them in age. The thing about being very young is that you're far more likely to stick to the books and worry about it far more, especially with the first, although that could partly have been because I wasn't near my mother.

And I was much more inclined to be hostile to any ideas put forward by other people.

'I enjoy having a grown-up — well, semi-grown-up — daughter, I suppose purely for the egotistical reason of people saying, "But you can't possibly have a daughter of that age," like the Palmolive advert. I suppose it means you remember more vividly the sort of things you got annoyed with your parents for when you were a teenager and perhaps that makes you more receptive. I never understand women who say they feel jealous of their daughters. I quite like it when I see men looking admiringly at Claudia.

'Claudia knows that I was pregnant with her when I got married. I always wanted to tell her that rather than anyone else tell her, but I think she knew anyway. She was 14 or 15 when I told her. She said, "But you would have got married anyway, wouldn't you?" so I said yes we would. I wouldn't like Claudia to have a baby so young — it would mean her marrying this year and having a child next spring, to be the equivalent of me. I wouldn't like her to do it, I think it's a mistake. But you can't tell other people.'

Like Helen, Pippa was quite pleased to discover she was pregnant at the age of 17; her mother, on the other hand, was dismayed, and coerced her into a marriage which broke up a few years later. Because she knew she needed her mother's help if she was to continue with her career, Pippa, who is now 29, complied.

'When I got pregnant I don't think it was an accident as such. I knew exactly how not to get pregnant, and I'd seen my sister have a child without marriage and support in that respect, so I knew it could be done. And I knew that if I did have a child I could still carry on with my A levels. I was quite aware of what was involved when I did it, and if I really hadn't wanted to have the baby, I would have had the pregnancy terminated. It would have been possible without her finding out.

'Mum's attitude was you've got to get married. I did because I thought she would be more compliant, and I knew that she would help me look after the child so that I could carry on doing what I wanted to do. I remember her crying and saying, "I thought it would never happen to you. You always told me you'd wait until you got married." She automatically assumed that I'd been raped, or that there'd been some unfortunate one time when I'd given in and she was having to deal with the consequence. She couldn't accept that I had an active sex life, and had done for about three years.

'Mum really wanted me to go to university because my brothers and sister hadn't, but she wanted me to get married as well. From an early age she used to talk about what the wedding would be like, what kind of hat she'd wear, and who I would have as a bridesmaid. We'd spend quite a lot of time looking through magazines at wedding dresses.

'In the event I did have a big wedding, though not a white one. Mum didn't have to keep saying that she was disappointed because it was obvious. I got married entirely because of the pressure from her. She bullied me into it. And the baby's father didn't want to get married. She said to him, "If you don't get married, we're leaving and you'll never see Pippa again." It was all to do with what the neighbours would think. With me it was the knowledge that she wouldn't support me, she'd be absolutely no help unless I did what she wanted; it would just be this ongoing resentment that I'd seen with my elder sister, who had been in the same position as me but hadn't got married to the father.

'Yet getting closer to mum has been to do with having children myself. She can come out with pearls of wisdom that are just to do with experience. She's quite good company now. She's always had a really good sense of humour which is quite a strength; it tends to lessen the pressure.'

6.
OLDER MOTHERS AND GRANDMOTHERS

'I do think about the age gap but I dismiss it out of hand. As far as adolescence goes, I really think that it's the person that matters, it's nothing to do with age.'

Yvonne

'I first became aware that mum was older when I went to school and I saw what the other mothers were like. That's when I started saying my granny would pick me up from school, so that no comments like "Isn't she old?" would arise I suppose. I don't think I felt embarrassed, although I must have been.'

Pippa

These days, the tendency is for more and more women to start families later in life than previous generations would have considered desirable, or even possible before contraception became widely available. Increasing numbers of women these days make a conscious decision to get career and relationships on an even keel before taking on the responsibility of children. Many women feel that they just aren't mature enough to bring up a child in their early twenties; they may also want to see a bit of life before they settle down.

There are obvious advantages to delaying a family until your thirties or even forties; a woman with an established career is unlikely to feel she's missing out, and she's also more likely to be able to return to work if she wants to. In turn, older couples tend to have fewer financial worries.

But there are disadvantages too. Older women often find it more difficult to conceive in the first place, and if there's a need to seek medical help for infertility, they may find that it's too late. Older women tend to have more difficult births, they run a higher risk of conceiving a Down's syndrome baby, and they tend to have less energy to cope with the demands of young children.

And, in fear of stating the obvious, there's a wider age gap between mother and child. It seemed to me that a big age gap might have particular significance in relationships between mothers and daughters, lessening the level of understanding and sympathy during the often difficult teenage years and beyond, in short, emphasising the generation gap. As Roberta put it, 'My mother was in her forties when she had me and it was like being brought up by your grandparents. We had to be in at ridiculously early times like 9.30. If I was five minutes late there would be a terrible row. She was very strict.' After all, most women find that the older they get, the more difficult it is to remember what it was like to be a teenager. We either remember all the bad things or all the good.

And don't older mothers run the risk of saddling their daughters with the burden of looking after them in their dotage? In this chapter, women on both sides of the generation gap, a mother whose 2-year-old was born when she was 39, and a 29-year-old whose mother was 40 when she was born, consider what a big age difference has meant to them.

The second part of the chapter focuses on grandmothers: women who were brought up by their grandmothers and grandmothers who are bringing up granddaughters talk about a relationship which is inevitably affected by a generation gap, and yet which can often be more clear-sighted and fulfilling than the relationship between mother and daughter, simply because it is less emotionally charged.

Yvonne's daughter, Kirsty, was born when she was 39, after a previous miscarriage. She went back to work when

Kirsty was 6 months old. Thanks to her own mother's example in having Yvonne at the age of 37, Yvonne had few qualms about having a daughter in her late thirties.

Yvonne's reasons for starting a family late in life were fundamentally practical: she had a good career in management for British Telecom, and Kirsty's father was her second husband. But as she explains, there were very strong gut feelings which had put her off motherhood until she reached her late thirties: 'I didn't want to have a baby when I was younger; I just didn't feel maternal. It was something I decided when I was about 14 or 15, and I had an aunt who had a lot of children. She didn't have much money, and I saw what having lots of kids meant.

'I still don't really feel maternal in the strict sense of the word. I get bored looking after Kirsty all the time; I can cope with it two days a week.

'I don't think you begrudge the sacrifices at an older age. And I think that, having seen all your friends having children, you realise what it will be like. Materially you've probably got yourself sorted out and in that way there are no sacrifices; we'd got to the point where we had a lovely home and a lovely life and we wanted to share it. I think younger mothers are more worried about looking after their babies than enjoying them.

'When I told my mother we were going to be parents she assumed we were adopting a baby. When she realised I was pregnant at such an advanced age her reaction was "Oh dear". She was 37 when she had me, but she'd had children before; she only perceives the first child as a major event. She said, "You've left it very late to start," the implication being that there would be two or three trundling along after Kirsty. I'm not so sure! I would like another one for Kirsty, because the way we've chosen to continue to live may mean that she's a bit lonely. It would be different if she had a sister or brother to moan about us to when she's older.

'I do think about the age gap but I dismiss it out of hand, because since I can remember thinking about relationships with parents I have been adamant that you shouldn't have children to look after you in your old age. It's nice if it happens, but you shouldn't presume. What you can't control is the sense of responsibility the child has.

'As far as adolescence goes, I really think that it's the person that matters, it's nothing to do with age. My parents were quite old when I was a teenager, but they were marvellous. They might not be very modern or in touch with the world, but there wasn't anything I asked that they didn't answer, and they always tried to understand. But then perhaps I was an over-reasonable teenager! I can't imagine what I'm going to be like in 15 years' time; if I'm still at work I'll probably be more in touch with what's going on.'

Pippa is the youngest of four children: she has two brothers 17 and 15 years older, and a sister nine years older. Her mother made a positive decision to have another baby, Pippa, when she was 40. Pippa is now 29 and has three sons. As a child, she says she was more bothered by the loneliness of her position in the family than by her mother's age. Although she never felt consciously embarrassed by it, she was obviously aware of some sort of stigma, since she used to fend off adverse comments by referring to her as granny. The age difference affected her more as an adolescent, when a real rift in understanding developed.

'I first became aware that mum was older when I went to school and I saw what the other mothers were like. I was aware that they were younger; that's when I started saying my granny would pick me up from school. I referred to my parents as granny and grandad to my friends so that no questions or comments, like "Isn't she old?", would arise, I suppose.

'Mum found out when a teacher asked her if she was my granny — it seems awful, doesn't it? — and mum said, "No, Pippa hasn't got any grandparents." The teacher said, "Oh well, it must be wishful thinking," and that's how it was palmed off.

'I don't think I felt embarrassed, although I must have been. It was just that she was different, and it was a lot to do with what she looked like — fat, with permed hair and things. That got worse at boarding school because there the mothers did tend to be pretty glamorous and that was the issue rather than her age. But before that it was because she was old.

'I used to think the fact that she didn't understand me was to do with her age. That's what I thought at the time, but having met women with good relationships with their mothers regardless of the age difference I realise it's nothing to do with that. Her attitude was definitely alienating, but I don't think it was necessarily because of her age. We were in different worlds. She didn't understand what was going on. There was one time when I got really into my A levels and I can remember spending a whole afternoon reading *Othello*; it was the greatest thing I'd ever read. At the end of that afternoon she was really worried that there was something wrong with me, that I was in some deep depression. Her answer to that was to go up to the school to find out why I had gone all funny.

'Lots of my friends would be able to talk to their parents about going on the Pill and so on, but there was no way I could confront that kind of thing. We never talked about contraception and sex. She would say things like, "You've got to let boys know that you've got it but you mustn't let them have it, and you've got to have a white wedding," all that kind of stuff.

'I was always aware of the fact that it was indulgent having a child at that age, that I was required for company. She's always said that she was pleased, that I did fulfil that role. I never got the impression that being older bothered her.

'But for me, the overwhelming thing was loneliness. My mother describes a scene, which she obviously found endearing, of me sitting on the doorstep talking to my imaginary friend. She thought it was sweet and a nice thing to watch. I remember that exact scene but feeling really lonely. I don't remember the special friend; we have completely different images of the same experience.

'My having a child at 17 was definitely to do with that

loneliness. I wanted a child to keep me company. When I was about 14 I used to take the dogs for a walk on the beach every Sunday afternoon, and I remember wishing that I had a little boy with me. I managed to fend that off for a few years — I didn't get pregnant until I was 17.' (Now in her late sixties, Pippa's mother suffers from Parkinson's disease; Pippa talks more about the effect of the illness on their relationship in Chapter 9, Role Reversal.)

Gerda, 42, is German and has lived in Derbyshire since she was a teenager. Until then she was brought up in Germany by her grandmother, who is now 85. She has fond memories of her upbringing, and a great deal of respect for the philosophy her grandmother instilled in her. They have always been close but not in the way that Gerda and her younger daughter Rachel are. For the age gap undoubtedly gave rise to misunderstandings and a basic lack of communication between grandmother and granddaughter, which wasn't helped by the unwelcome arrival of a step-grandfather and Gerda's bitterness towards the mother who had abandoned her.

'My mother was divorced soon after I was born. She left for England and I was brought up by my grandmother. When I was 16 my mother decided she wanted me. There'd been no communication, no telephone calls, no letters, no visits, nothing, then out of the blue she decided she wanted this daughter and took me out of my environment, away from my school friends and brought me to England. I resented this something chronic. Perhaps it hasn't all come out yet. We constantly rowed, you can't imagine the near fights we had.

'And yet now I feel compelled to visit her because my grandmother is now living with her. I look upon my grandmother as my mother really, so I've got this terrible urge to visit my mother just to visit my grandmother. But after half an hour with my mother I'm itching to go.

'My relationship with my grandmother has influenced my relationship with my daughters. She was very strict, but she never told me anything. I started my periods very

young and I thought, what the hell's this? I told her I'd
messed my underwear and I couldn't figure out her reaction at all: all she said was "I want to see that every
month". When I asked her why, she said, "You'll get to
know sooner or later," but she never told me.

'I respect my grandmother tremendously. She ruled me
with an iron rod, but she was always kind, and she was a
very practical person. The only shortcoming she had was
that I couldn't talk to her. I thought, if ever I have children, they must be able to get through to me and vice
versa.

'I've survived the difficult periods in my life — I've been
divorced twice and at the moment I'm thousands of
pounds in debt — thanks to my grandmother's upbringing. I think if I'd been brought up by my mother I would
never have survived; I would have taken an overdose or
run away or done something silly, because I wouldn't have
been able to cope. She had this tremendous philosophy;
she used to say, "Whatever life throws at you, you'll cope
with it. That's what you're here for".'

Alison has brought up her eldest granddaughter,
Mandy, who is now 8, and her grandson, Craig, almost
continuously since Mandy was a baby. Mandy lived for
short periods of her life with her mother, Alison's
daughter, Michelle, who was 15 when Mandy was born.
When Alison discovered that Mandy was being abused by
her mother and stepfather, she managed, after a long legal
battle during which Mandy was in care and in foster
homes, to become her legal guardian. Unless the situation
changes dramatically, Mandy will stay with her grandparents until she's grown up.

Alison has evidently been deeply hurt by the break with
her daughter (this is described in more detail in Chapter 7)
and the only contact they have these days is when
Michelle rings up to speak to Mandy.

The bond between Alison and Mandy has been strong
since Mandy's birth, at which Alison was present. It was
reinforced by Alison's sympathy for her granddaughter's
terrible suffering: there were nearly 50 recorded inci-

dents of abuse. Her relationship with Mandy must in some way make up for the daughter Alison has, effectively, lost, although at times she has been torn between the two.

'I was there when Mandy was born, and I think that's why there's such a bond between us. I've had four children of my own but I couldn't tell you what the birth was about. To me, actually being there and seeing her born was the most wonderful thing in my life. It really was a thrill.

'My other daughter and I are like sisters, and I'm hoping I'll have that sort of relationship with Mandy because she can always come and talk to me about anything. Michelle never has. She lives in a complete dream world. We've never really had anything at all, Michelle and I, right the way through. As a child she never sat in a room with the rest of the family and watched television, or played a game, she always wanted to be on her own in her room doing her own thing.

'Deep down, obviously, she's still my daughter and I would love to see her settle down and things work out for her. But I don't really want her involved with me. All the time I've got the fear that she could get control over the two children.

'To begin with I worried more about the age gap between Mandy and me than I do now. My mother, who is 83, had my sister when she was 45, so it does happen that you have a child at that age. I was quite taken aback by having two children to look after at that time of my life, but I thought, if my mother could bring up my sister on her own, with no help or support, there's no reason why I can't. I'm 50 this year, but I don't feel my age, and I suppose I'm very aware of the age gap so I do try to get involved a lot more. I try to do everything with Mandy that a mother normally does with her daughter — I go swimming with her, tap dancing, ballet, I sit and play games with her. Maybe she gets far more attention from me than she would from a mother who was younger.

'I often wonder what Mandy is going to grow up like, is she going to be like her mother or like my other daughter, who is very close to me; I've never had a day's trouble with her. The psychiatrist told me that the way to explain the situation to Mandy was that there were two sets of parents, one to bring her into the world and one to look after her. She said I should try and tell her the good bits about both her parents, and not the bad bits, because later on in life it would affect her. But really it's a hard job because at times, even now, I say, "Ooh, you're just like your mother." It just comes out, there are things you just can't stop saying. On the whole I've tried to explain to her that Michelle was only at school and she didn't know how to look after her.

'I've made up my mind that Mandy won't go to an all girls' school, like her mother did. From a very young age, all Michelle thought about was getting into boys' company, that's all she wanted, boys, boys, boys. The thing with Michelle was that she grew up too quickly and that's what I'm hoping won't happen to Mandy. Michelle had a 36 inch bust when she was 12.

'I think Mandy's marvellous. When I first had her she used to hide, but now she's very confident, even though she's overweight, she dances and she put on a big show last Friday. I'm very proud that she's overcome the past and that she's got confidence and she's got a mind of her own.

'She can't remember the foster homes, but she can remember what was done to her. Little things still come back to her. You can't turn out the lights in her bedroom, and everything has to be just where she puts it. Before she gets into bed everything has to go back in the right place. Whether it was because she lived in such squalor before or whether it's to stop her seeing a shadow that she's not expecting when she wakes up, I don't know.

'We all felt so much for her and we all tried to make up for what she'd lost, although we've been told you can't do that. In fact now we are finding it a bit hard with discipline, because we've given in so much. Smacking her wouldn't be the answer, she's been through all that.

'To start with there was no problem at the school about me looking after her. The other mums and for some reason the other children didn't ask questions. It's now she's in the juniors that it's started to come out. At dancing class the other day, one of the other little girls said to her, "Why don't you live with your mum?" She said, "Well, it's a long story and I don't want to go into it now." The little girl said, "Did her mum have a heart attack?", so I said no, she just couldn't look after her so her nanny looks after her. We leave it at that.

'She does get upset about access. She said she didn't want her mum going to the school because she'd have to explain to her teachers and her friends what role her mum took in her life. As long as it's in the school holidays she's quite happy about going, but if it interferes with her daily routine she doesn't want to know.

'At times I do feel resentful about having a second set of kids to look after, and then my husband gets it in the ear, I've got to admit. When I get in one of those moods I sit here saying I've never achieved anything in my life, all I've had is kids. I used to go out to bingo and I used to be in a darts team, but now I don't do that kind of thing. I've been out three times since Mandy came to live with us. But I don't resent it really, because the children coming along late has done a lot for me. My husband was already ill when they first came, he had started to be a bit of a cabbage and I was getting to be one too. I was just sitting there in the afternoon and going to sleep. But I never planned it that way, to steal my daughter's children from her. I think your life's mapped out for you by someone out there, I'm convinced of it.'

7.
ARGUMENTS, CONFLICT AND CRISIS; MENOPAUSAL MOTHERS

'What's shocked my mother has always been to do with sexual relationships. When I was 15 we were at church one Sunday morning and she wanted to introduce me to someone. Apparently I had a love bite on my neck and when I got home she wouldn't speak to me. She left me a note — that's what she always did, she wrote me letters.'

Pippa

'She screamed and shouted at us and it was as if she was a complete stanger. I couldn't dream that anybody could speak to us like that; I've never shouted at my mother in my life.'

Alison

Arguments provide a key to relationships between mothers and daughters. Every mother has arguments with her daughter, indeed they're usually a healthy sign. As one divorced mother said, rather ruefully, 'Any divorced parent will tell you that they have a very unnatural relationship with the children that they don't live with, and it's only when you start having rows with children that you're back to a normal relationship.' She argued rarely with her 13-year-old daughter; the problem was getting any form of communication going.

The majority of the women I spoke to said they argued most about housework, even if they no longer lived together; boyfriends and potential husbands also came high on the hit list. It's hardly surprising that rows tend to be sparked off by mundane issues like housework, since relationships between mothers and daughters are the stuff of everyday life — issues like whether the house is tidy are important, because it's women who take care of the minutiae of life. Occasionally the roles are reversed — Rachel, for example, is always getting furious with her mother's lack of domestication, which in itself seems to be a symbol of her mother's new-found freedom. When she was married she conformed totally to the image of the perfect housewife and mother.

The tricky subject of men — so often a bone of contention — takes on a special importance for many Asian mothers and their daughters, like Angela, who describes her own return to the fold after a long period of rejecting all things Asian when her mother was deeply depressed after another daughter had married an Englishman.

It's a sad fact that while some arguments are a good way of clearing the air, others cause a permanent rift. The bond between mother and daughter is such that conflicts which remain totally unresolved are rare. A total breakdown in communication can last years, but reconciliation is always possible, even probable. But the rift between Alison and her daughter Michelle seems permanent. Their conflict over Michelle's daughter ended with a lengthy legal battle and total estrangement.

And, of course, there are arguments and arguments. One woman's furious row is another woman's petty squabble. Gerda and Rachel's constant banter about housework is essentially jolly, and it serves its purpose, keeping them both on an even keel during a very difficult period of debt, depression and loneliness. Oddly enough, it gives an impression of intimacy, of the two women united against the rest of the world.

With Maureen and her daughter, Maxine, it's more like the kind of bickering you see over and over again with teenage daughters and their mothers, the mother offering suggestions, the daughter quick to contradict. There is a tense edge to their conversation which shows that, close as they are, their personalities grate on each other. And hardly surprisingly, since they're both unemployed, they're both stuck at home and Maureen's horrified — who wouldn't be? — to see her daughter's life going to waste in a daily ritual of endless baths, trips to the pub, and videos in the afternoon. Maureen's menopause hasn't helped matters; later, she and two other women talk about the effect of menopause on their relationship with their daughters.

Many mothers, like Roberta, eventually come to the conclusion that the only way to get over a prolonged period of disagreement is to compromise. In Roberta's case, the change all came from her side, but it's had the desired effect. Jenny and Roberta don't have one of those idealised, sisterly friendships so many women long for, but they do get on better than they used to.

It's part of growing up — a process involving both mother and daughter — to move away from a relationship where the mother calls the tune. Yet mother nagging, daughter complying with a self-pitying groan, is a pattern so tightly woven into the fabric of our relationships, that it can be difficult to get away from a degree of pointless bickering in adult relationships with mothers. I've often heard women say they're consumed with guilt because on the last visit to their mother they went with the best intentions but yet again, after ten minutes the conversation disintegrated into the usual tension and impatience. It's almost as if the way women behave with their mothers is out of their control, in a way that never happens with other relationships, with the obvious exception of lovers. Perhaps this is the daughter's vengeance, now that she's in a position of power, for all those years of being told to brush her hair, wash her hands and behave nicely. More probably it's that for many mothers and daughters, it's impossible to completely break away from the rhythms of the relationship established in childhood.

Jenny, now away at medical school in Edinburgh, has never had an easy relationship with her mother, Roberta, and things took a distinct turn for the worse when Jenny's father died suddenly when she was 17 and her mother was 39. Jenny, the eldest of three daughters, was sent back to boarding school a week after her father's death; five years on, she still says it's something she finds difficult to forgive. Roberta, who lives outside Glasgow, thinks that in retrospect it was probably a mistake, but at the time she didn't know what to do for the best.

'She needed to go back for the work,' she says. 'The three other children were at home with me and we grieved together. We all slept together for a long time and we were aware of each other all the time, and all the people calling and so on. Jenny was away from this and when she came back at Christmas I think she'd almost pretended it hadn't happened and she was so bolshy and so difficult. She was stroppy even when Donald was alive, but he handled her very well; they were very close. She didn't want to know me, she didn't want to know any of us; she was frustrated and difficult and angry. She was so rude to me and I didn't know how to handle it. I reacted badly too; I used to say I can't cope with you at home, I just can't stand it. Then gradually she got better and now she's fine.

'I think the reason that Jenny and I are getting on better now is not because she's changed but because I've changed. I think I'm less demanding and more tolerant than I used to be. I realised that if I carried on the way I was I wouldn't have seen Jenny again. There was no way I could impose my will on her. Somebody had to bend and give in. I didn't cope very well when Donald died and I don't think she did either. But I think she's grown up a lot. These days she's very nice to have around.'

For Jenny the period after her father died was equally traumatic: 'I've never forgiven my mum for sending me back to boarding school; I just wasn't ready to go back. I really didn't want to be in a place that I didn't particularly like anyway. To be put back there when they were all still at home was really hard. I used to beg mum to let me stay at home, but she would be having none of it; I felt very unfairly done towards. I think mum thought I hadn't taken it as hard as I had. In fact I was just as upset as everyone else. She used to say, "It's all right for you, you can just dismiss it," but that wasn't true at all. I think she still thinks that I've got a heart of stone.

'When we have a disagreement, we have a big row and then she doesn't speak for three days. We don't ever fall out small, it's always big. We can both be incredibly bad mooded. If I go home we get on very well for four or five days and then comes the crisis point. Either she starts yelling at me for trying to rearrange her house or for not wanting to do what she wants to do. She used to expect me to go to school concerts and things with her, and I didn't feel I should have to — I suppose that's unreasonable as well. She saw the priority as family whereas I didn't.

'When I was still living at home I argued a lot with mum, about clothes, what you did when you went out and so on. I think she wanted me to go out more than I did, she wanted me to be more in with the group. It was always mum rather than dad who set the rules about being in on time. I know now that it was because she was worried about me, but I didn't at the time. But the worst arguments I had were after I'd left home.

'I was always a bit late, but there was one time when I was 18 when I was particularly late and she threw me out and locked me out of the house. She threw all my belongings out and said, "You're leaving." It was New Year's Eve and she'd said I'd to be in by midnight. I rang at about 10 and pleaded with her to let me come in at half past 12 and she said no. I came back after 2 and she was absolutely furious.

'I knew I'd be in trouble but I thought if I'm a bit late I'll get into trouble, so it won't make much difference being a lot later. When I got home she'd locked the house, so I went and stayed with a friend and went home the following morning. She'd left a note on the door saying, "You're not living here any more if you can't get in by midnight." She had a complete and utter fit, threw everything out of the door and said I might as well get on the train. I went to a friend's house, and her mum said I should go back and apologise, which I did. But mum wasn't listening to reason at that stage — I still don't think she was being reasonable. So I went back to my friend's house, and mum thought I had got on the train so she sent all the relatives to the station in Glasgow and through to Edinburgh to look for me. When I went home in the afternoon, all tearful, she told me to ring my aunt and uncle to apologise to them for the inconvenience. I did but I still didn't think it was my fault. Mum was quite unrepentant; I've never forgiven her for it. It was awful having to apologise for something that wasn't my fault.'

Arguments about men can be the most painful for both sides. The chances are that a mother will never think any man is good enough for her daughter, and equally, the daughter is unlikely to take a blind bit of notice of her advice, however carefully phrased. It can be hard to admit your mother is right, even in retrospect. Gerda, now 42, had a major row with her mother because she made no attempt to disguise her dislike of Gerda's first husband: 'My mum was dead against me marrying him. She completely cut herself off from me. She said, "If you marry him, don't bother coming up here if you've got any problems." We were never close anyway so it didn't matter. Now that my husband and I are no longer together she does get on with him, strangely enough.

'I still find my mother a strain. As much as I try, when you talk to her you might as well be talking to that cabinet. She's not interested in what you have to say, but you must listen to what she's telling you, although what she's talking about is the woman down the road's third cousin twice removed. You can't hold a conversation like that for more than ten minutes.

'With my own daughters I used to argue about boyfriends. The boy Rachel ran away with, I completely and utterly disliked, and for good reason, but Rachel couldn't see it at the time. I used to try and tell her that he was no good, and there would be fireworks. But then of course she found out, because he hit her once or twice and I think slowly but surely it began to dawn.'

But the biggest row Gerda and Rachel have had in a long time was a three-generation affair, and like so many arguments, its trigger was painfully trivial. Significantly, it was precipitated by Gerda's mother and elder daughter and highlights the tensions between the women in the family.

Rachel remembers: 'The last real bust-up was after me and my boyfriend had been to a nightclub in Matlock and we were walking up the road to flag a taxi down. My sister saw us and she told my gran she'd seen us hitch-hiking. When my mum saw her gran said, "Did you know your daughter was walking home at a quarter to three in the morning?"'

Gerda continued, 'It was the way she put it — the implication was, I hope you realise what your daughter's up to while you're not there. It was a jibe at me staying with my boyfriend on Saturday night. I went bananas.'

Rachel describes the scene: 'She came flying through that door with a face like stone saying, "I want a word with you." That's fatal; I hate it when she says that. She was so angry she didn't listen to my side of the story. Normally she's not like that. It's my gran, she really winds her up.' Gerda realised how angry she was. 'Rachel swore at me, she used the "f" word. I said, "I'll kill you, you bitch," and I got hold of her — we nearly came to blows. She walked out of the front door. By the time she came back about an hour later, we'd both calmed down and I listened to her side of the story. And then we were all right.'

The worst row Yvonne and her mother ever had was also about a man. In retrospect, like Rachel, she discovered her mother had been right: 'I had a good relationship with my mother. We only ever had one dreadful row and that was about my first husband. She never ever said, I told you so, but she knew what he was before I did. The row was dreadful, not so much because she thought this man was no good for me in certain ways, but because I said some cruel things about my dad, like "Well, you didn't make such a good catch, did you?" She found that so hurtful, she couldn't accept that in my temper I was grabbing at anything that would hurt. She felt it must have been inside me waiting to come out, and that I really didn't respect my father.'

Pippa's arguments with her mother have always been to

do with sex. And she believes that her mother's practice of leaving notes and sulking has left its mark on the way she deals with disagreements with other people.

'What's shocked my mother has always been to do with sexual relationships. When I was about 15, we were at church one Sunday morning and she wanted to introduce me to someone. Apparently I had a love bite on my neck (I didn't even know it was there) and when I got home she wouldn't speak to me. She left a note saying how disappointed she was with me, that she'd felt proud, and wanted to introduce me and then she'd noticed this thing on my neck and she'd been totally humiliated. That's what she always did, she wrote me letters. I'd go up to my bedroom and there'd be a letter. It was always stuff like, you've failed me, you've let me down, I've done my best and this is how you repay me. It made me feel terrible, I believed her, I thought I really had failed her. It hit home, and I think I carry it with me, this fear of failure.

'I tried to talk to her about it on a couple of occasions, but she'd look completely the other way. So I had to write a letter back to her — it's unbelievable, isn't it?

'I'd try and get through at first, but she would sulk so then it would just be us ignoring each other for a few days. These days I sulk with my husband, in fact it's more than a sulk, it's like recoil — I just can't utter a word, sometimes for as long as twenty-four hours. I definitely picked that up from my mum, that it's easier to avoid an issue than confront it.'

In Angela's family, disagreements have often focused on men. Pressure from the Asian community reinforced Angela's mother's violent opposition to the idea of any of her five daughters marrying an English person. Two of her daughters have married Englishmen, which Angela's mother has found very difficult to come to terms with.

Angela, who is now 36, also went through a long period of rejecting all things Asian, from adolescence onwards, and was regarded by the community as totally anglicised, and highly likely to follow in her two sisters' footsteps. Yet her marriage to her Asian boyfriend ten years ago was partly an attempt to counteract her mother's deep depression following the first daughter's marriage.

She explains why she even went for the full ritual of a traditional ceremony: 'The reason why I wanted to go through this traditional marriage was that it would give mum something to do. I felt it was time for her to try and forget my sister's situation, and to get her mind diverted into something else.' It's a touching example of an attempt to set wrongs to right by a fairly dramatic and very public expression of faith in the things that really matter to a mother. But in Angela's case, it almost backfired, because 'To this day, mum says I rushed into marriage. She thinks that it's her fault, that if she hadn't been so depressed, and hadn't been so preoccupied with my sister, that I wouldn't have got married. But as I often say to mum, no matter who we married they'd never be good enough for you.

'My mum really has lived her life through us. A typical Asian, sacrificing mother is what I would put her down as. The last person she thinks about is herself. But because of the sacrifices she's made, the demands tend to be quite high.'

Angela's mother's fears for her daughters have their roots in the past, as Angela explains: 'Everyone advised my parents not to bring five girls to this country, because they thought we would all marry Englishmen and all become awful. It was regarded as lunacy to go to England, where your children would lose all culture.

'After a while, as more and more Asians started to come to this country, we started to get a community feeling, but mum noticed that we were drifting away from our culture and that worried her. What everybody had warned her about was happening. We all went through rebellious stages. You know how as a teenager you go through the stage of rejecting everything that is you. I went through the stage of thinking I didn't want anything to do with anything Asian. I had English friends, and an English boyfriend who wanted to marry me. We went through a lot of racism at school, the outcome of which was that I started rejecting my own people. I thought if I became like the English, they would accept me. So I tried to discard completely what I was and become somebody I wasn't. I think I must have been quite wicked to my mother. Somebody once said that I was the last person they thought would marry an Asian person, because I had become so anglicised, that the thought that I would ever come back was impossible.

'When my elder sister ran away from home and sent a letter saying she was married, my mother was completely shellshocked. She didn't tell the community; she didn't admit it to other people for a long time. So when I got married the community couldn't understand why the younger daughter was getting married before the older one. My sister would make appearances where necessary, she came to my marriage for example, but on her own. But my mother asked her to go and live somewhere where she wouldn't be seen. Things seemed to ease up when my sister's daughter was born, but I don't think mum will ever 100 per cent accept it. It's the way she was brought up: I can understand it now I have children of my own.

'My younger sister has also married an Englishman, and although my mother hasn't told anyone else, and none of us went to the marriage, she has reacted better than I thought she would. But my younger sister didn't go behind mum's back, that was the big difference.

'My elder sister got married behind my mother's back; it was all the lying and the cheating that mum found hard to take. My mother's feelings are always up front; you always know what she's feeling. My younger sister confronted my parents with it and my mother respects her for that. She said she didn't feel like an Asian person, because she came here when she was only 11 months old. Because she talked to mum about it, even though it hurt mum and they cried and hugged and went through the painful process of it all, in lots of ways it's brought them a lot closer.'

Alison's daughter, Michelle, got pregnant when she was 15 with her daughter Mandy. When the child was a toddler, Alison realised that she was being abused by her mother and stepfather and when Mandy was 3, Alison applied to have her made a ward of court. After a long legal battle, during which mother and daughter met only in court,

Alison was made her granddaughter's legal guardian. Mandy was 5 by this time. Even before this, Alison's relationship with her daughter had been very difficult, but Alison's attempts to help and understand were shattered by the violence of the clash over Mandy.

For Alison the most difficult thing has always been resisting her daughter's persistent attempts to make peace, particularly now that Michelle is pregnant again, and swears that she is turning over a new leaf. It must be heartbreaking for any mother to reject a child. But Alison has good reason: she has lost all trust in her daughter, and if she does give in to her, she risks losing her grandchildren. Alison has no choice but to transfer her affections lock, stock and barrel to her granddaughter. These days, Alison speaks to Michelle on the phone, but only if she has to.

'To start with, it made me very, very sad. The Christmas after I had Mandy, Michelle was in a battered women's home. She phoned me on Christmas morning. To think that anybody, it doesn't matter if they're a complete stranger, is on their own on Christmas morning without anything, is really ghastly, but when it's a child you brought into the world, and you brought up. ... But there was no way I could give in to her because I would have lost my rights to the children. My heart went out to her and if I'd given in to my heart I could have ruined everything. Now I just don't want to get involved with her. I just don't want to know because it hurts too much.

'The first couple of times I saw her in court, she was so thin. She weighed 6 or 7 stone. She'd been on drugs, and she looked so tarty. Then the hatred started coming, when she screamed and shouted at us in court. I just sat there and she was screaming and shouting at us and it was as if she was a complete stranger, she just didn't belong to us. I couldn't dream that anybody could speak to us like that; I've never shouted at my mother in my life and I still wouldn't, I've got far too much respect for her even now. The things she said and the way she acted to us was just like a stranger.

'I've never been able to express what I felt inside and

now when I see her, as soon as I know she's coming, I get that horrible cold feeling inside. I don't want to see her. I just don't want to talk to her, and she is trying so hard to talk to us. She's done this so many times to us, that I've got no trust in her at all. I'm always thinking, well, what are you going to do to us next.

'I try to put myself in her place sometimes and think if I met somebody I really cared for, like she's supposed to have done now, and she's having another baby, I'd move out of the district. She could set up a new life in a place where no one would know her at all, with no social worker to come and take the child away, no interfering mother. . . .

'To start off with I could understand Michelle because I'd done the same kind of thing when I was young, although I was a lot older than her at the time. I'd met the wrong man, I'd gone the wrong way — I think I had the shortest marriage on record, it only lasted a week. I was the black sheep of the family. Up until I was 20 everything was lovely, but from then on things started snowballing. I was a bit of a rebel myself then. I left my husband after a week to live with another man, and my dad died three months later. My family decided that it was me who killed him. My mum didn't speak to me for 18 months, until my first daughter was born. My mother still says the only reason you came in this house again was over your dad's dead body. I've got used to it now, but for years and years I used to cry my eyes out about it.

'Deep down, obviously, Michelle is still my daughter and I would love to see her settle down and things work out for her. But I don't really want her involved with me. All the time I've got the fear that she could get control over these two [children]. You just can't wash out what she's done to Mandy; you can't just say she was immature. I mean she was old enough to have sex, she was old enough to have the baby. She told me I was interfering and to leave her alone. Why should we just forget all that and say it's hard luck? She had plenty of people to look after her and she just didn't want to know. She abused everything everybody gave to her.'

Diane and her daughter, Sarah, don't row often, and when they do it's very upsetting, particularly to Sarah, who's always hated shouting. Diane describes a recent row, which obviously distressed her very much, although as with so many rows, the cause was a trivial misunderstanding. In fact it hit a nerve on both sides. The row focussed on Diane's psychotherapy group, which Sarah disapproves of; she thinks it gives her mother 'some funny ideas'. No wonder it gave rise to such extreme reactions on both sides.

Diane says, 'I got quite upset in my psychotherapy group and I came home and I don't think Sarah took in that I was upset and she started mimicking my facial expressions. I got very, very angry with her and she cried and said, "For heaven's sake, can't anyone in this house take a joke?", and went up to her room in tears. I felt terrible, but I didn't go to her because my own internal feelings were still so high that I couldn't really talk to her at that point. I went to her a few hours later and I said, "I didn't mean to upset you, I was just upset myself." And we quickly sorted things out.'

At 50, Diane is in the throes of the menopause, but she has found that Hormone Replacement Therapy has kept the awful symptoms some women experience at bay. The positive attitude she has adopted was inspired by her problems with her own mother. 'My mother was extremely difficult to deal with during the menopause: I didn't know what on earth was going on most of the time. She was a difficult woman anyway and I was determined I was never going to be like her. My mother always looked old.'

It seems to have worked. Sarah says, 'I can never make up my mind whether Mum is going through the menopause or not. She doesn't talk to me about it. In fact I think she's less bad tempered than she used to be. She used to get quite annoyed about little things — like once I spilt a glass of milk and she was so annoyed. That's the first time I ever heard her swear at me. It was such a shock. Or if she had a bad day at work, she'd get really annoyed.'

Maureen, who is in her early forties, hasn't been so lucky; not only did she start to have menopausal symptoms unusually early, shortly after she was sterilised in her mid-thirties, but the menopause also coincided with other crises in her life. Her mother has become very dependent on her since she was widowed recently, and she was made redundant last year, so for the first time in her life she is without work outside the home. She admits she finds it very depressing. Her daughter, Maxine, is in the same boat. The menopause, and the fact that they're both unemployed, have had a dramatic effect on their relationship.

Maureen says, 'Maxine's idle, that's her biggest problem. She's not the way I was at her age. It frustrates me that she doesn't do anything. She's stupid really, because she's been out with a lad for five years and it's no good. He never takes her out; he comes round once a week and sits with her while she babysits. I don't call that going out. There's a lot more to life. Maxine hasn't seen any of it yet. I missed out on it and I don't want her to. I'm having quite a bad time with the change. I'm very nasty tempered because of that. I tell Maxine off all the time.'

Maxine confirms this, 'She tells me off when I haven't even done anything wrong. She'll shout before she knows anything about it — she'll blame me for something that either she's done herself or my dad's done and it's something dead trivial. So I have to shout back and call her all the names under the sun and say, get your facts right before you start shouting at me. Mum's a hypochondriac; she's got something wrong with her every day.' Maureen denies this. 'I'm not. That's what you're like when you're on the change; you ought to watch some of these programmes about it.' Maxine retorts, 'I've never known you not like it.'

'That's only because I've been on it since I was 35,' answers Maureen, 'and you started growing up and taking notice at that age. I've put 2 stone on, that's one of the things I can't cope with, I feel horrible. I'm not jealous of Maxine, I'm pig sick, because I love the clothes the young wear and I can't wear them. I feel ashamed of myself; I feel as if I've let myself go.'

Maxine says, 'I didn't realise she was going through the

change; I just thought she was really nasty. I thought there must be something desperately wrong with her head. I remember hearing comments in the street, like "I heard your mum shouting last night." It's so embarrassing; you're walking out in the street and she's still ranting on, having an argument with my dad or screaming at Mitchell and everyone's looking at you. But they don't understand what's going on.'

What they don't understand concerns Mitchell, Maxine's 17-year-old brother, who was severely brain damaged after a bout of meningitis at three months, and requires 24-hour care. Maureen says he has brought the family closer together, but the strain of looking after him has taken its toll on family life. The situation Maxine and Maureen now find themselves in would try the patience of a saint: they're both stuck at home, with no money and not many reasons to get up in the morning. As Maxine says, it's not surprising they get on each other's nerves, and the menopause doesn't help matters.

For Norma, the menopause has been equally traumatic — at times, she says, it's made her feel that she just can't cope. It's effectively driven a wedge between her and her two daughters, Suzanne, 30 and Karen, 27. They are painfully aware of a dramatic change in their mother, which they attribute either to the menopause, or to the Miners' Strike of 1984-5, in which Norma, the wife of a miner who has since been made redundant, was very active. For the first time, Norma had a life outside her family and was highly successful at things neither she, nor her husband and children, had ever dreamt she was capable of, from speaking at public meetings all over the country, to publishing a book. It brought about a revolution in Norma's thinking and way of life which, at times, her daughters found difficult to accept.

'My elder daughter, Suzanne, wasn't in agreement with the Strike because I'd brought her up to believe that the police were important and that violence was very, very wrong. Now all of a sudden, there's your mother against what the police are doing and not condemning the violence because we were fighting for something: she couldn't get that at all. I think she would rather we'd stopped at home until it was all over.

'All of a sudden she saw a different me, that she'd never seen before. It was something that I believed in that brought things out that I didn't know were in me. I think Suzanne thought I'd gone mental. We never actually fell out over it; she just told me one day that she didn't agree with it. She had her opinion and I had mine. But she still used to bring us groceries every week.

'Karen didn't have a lot to say about it, although I don't think she liked what I was doing. I don't suppose they like to think of their mother doing anything like that. I had always been so quiet and all of a sudden it was a different me.

'I don't think I'm as close to my daughters now as I used to be. They don't rely on me as much. When we all lived together we were a bit more like sisters because we used to be able to talk about things, and did things together — shopping, the pictures, or we'd go out for the day. I've always tried very hard not to interfere in their lives, because I wouldn't like it myself. So when things are going smoothly for them I keep in the background, but they know I'm there if they want me. I'm just somebody that's here when they need me. Now with our Karen at the moment I sometimes feel she needs me more than I can give her because I don't always feel 100 per cent myself now.

'I'm going through the change, and I get so that I can't cope properly. So although Karen really needs me, I don't feel able to give her what she needs. I've looked after the little boy for the night, but if she asked me to look after the kids for a day I'd panic. I don't suppose Karen is aware of it. I think they just think mothers should be there when they want them, that you should be all right.'

Karen, who looks after her four children on her own since she and her husband separated, had become used to a great deal of support, both emotional and practical, from her mother. But she feels that in the past four or five years, there's been a big change.

'When I first had Donna [who was born when Karen

was 16] and I still lived at home, I was closer to my mum, she was really protective. I don't know what I'd have done without her. I think that's what I miss now.

'I don't feel as though I'm as close to my mum as I used to be. I know she's there if I want her, but she's altered these last few years, she doesn't seem to be the same mum. Sometimes I go down and I feel as though she doesn't want me there, she doesn't really want to talk to me. Then some days she's different again.

'I think it was before the Strike that she started to alter. I know she didn't think much to Mick, the children's dad, but we still got on all right. I think it was when she started going through the change. She'd been to the doctor and I know she'd been poorly. Then when the Strike came I don't think that helped any. I think she got a bit worse. We just didn't see eye to eye on any subject. We used to go twice a week to the bingo together and shopping downtown and everything just stopped. She just didn't seem to want to spend any time with any of us.

'When you go down to visit her it takes her at least an hour to say hello to you, you feel as if she doesn't want you there. She doesn't even ask me about the man I've been seeing for the past six months. She doesn't want to meet him. If I tell her anything about him, she's just not interested. I stopped going down for a while because I felt that uncomfortable, and I didn't know what it was I'd done. I spoke to my sister about it and she said, she's the same with me. But if one of her friends from the village came to the house she'd perk herself up; it's as if it's just the family. The most irritating thing about mum is that she puts her friends before her family. It does hurt me and my sister a lot.

'It's two years since she came to see me. I started going down there once a week because I thought well, if I don't I'll never see her. But sometimes it seems such a trek with all the kids. Terry, my stepdad, is ever so good; he comes up and babysits for me. They've changed roles, I think. There are times when I get ever so depressed, I feel as if I'm on my own. I do wish I was closer to my mum than I am. She's just altered and I don't know why.'

8.
SEPARATION AND ADOPTION

'I felt I should be this mother that she wanted, but I didn't know how to do it. It's the same sort of thing as being given a new-born baby and thinking, O God, what do I do with it? It's almost like having a romantic liaison with someone you've never met before.'
> Gill, reunited with her daughter after 20 years.

'I never thought about finding my father, not once. It was purely a maternal thing. The maternal bond is such that you can't get away from it. It's too strong.'
> Susan, reunited with her birth mother after 28 years.

Long-term separation from a mother or daughter must be one of the most painful experiences life has to offer. Yet it provides intriguing clues to the nature of the bond between mothers and daughters, whether there's something innate that can survive a separation of say, twenty years, or whether it's the years of care and nurture that matter.

Karen and Susan, who were adopted as babies, both think the blood tie is sacrosanct. Gill, Karen's birth mother, is not convinced of its importance, although she acknowledges a close bond with Karen. Apart from anything else, there are physical resemblances — they look incredibly alike, have similar mannerisms, both suffer from flat feet and eczema. Karen says, 'I think the blood tie between mother and daughter is important. I know people say that's rubbish, that it's the relationship that you build when people are bringing you up that matters, but I really don't feel that way. I could be biased because I have a good relationship with my birth mother now. We're more like friends than mother and daughter.' Karen has also cut herself off completely from her adoptive mother.

Gill's experience has given her a different stance on blood ties: she was separated from her own mother during the formative early teenage years, and cites other women who cared for her as more satisfactory mother figures. When Karen first made contact with her four years ago, Gill set an ultimatum that she wouldn't meet Karen until she had made some attempt at reconciliation with her adoptive mother. Although Gill put an end to the ultimatum herself, she still sticks to her original line: 'I strongly believe that you have a responsibility to somebody who has looked after you, and whatever the difficulties are you can try and reconcile them. I try to explain to Karen that, irrespective of blood ties, there's a part of your life that has been shared with another person who will remember what you were like. Even if you were horrid, it doesn't matter, it's nice that someone cared enough to notice.

'There is a bond between me and Karen, although we don't know much about each other, because of those two and a half months I spent with her as a baby.'

But it's not easy to pick up the pieces after all those years apart, as Gill is the first to admit. Perhaps because she is older than Karen, Gill [who is 41; Karen is 24] has a much greater awareness of the emotional can of worms which Karen's arrival on the scene opened up. She feels Karen needs to face up to her feelings of resentment at being adopted, and regrets the fact that they had none of the careful counselling that most women in their situation are given to guide them through uncharted and often stormy waters. Ironically what maintains the distance between them is the characteristic they most obviously share, of bottling up their emotions. Neither Karen nor Gill feel they have the right to reach out to the other, and both are terrified of rejection.

Karen first rang Gill out of the blue, on a whim, when she was 16. After that she rang every few months for the next four years, when they finally met. Since then they've kept up regular contact.

Gill says, 'I felt tremendous pressure from Karen. I felt, this girl needs something that I can't give her; I don't know where to begin. I remember saying to her, "We live in a council house and I've got a very ill husband . . ." That poor girl at the other end of the phone. But if we'd had counselling, we'd have been carried through it in a much gentler way, to cope with all the things this door opened up.

'I felt I should be this mother that she wanted, but I didn't know how to do it. It's the same sort of thing as being given a new-born baby and thinking, O God, what do I do with it? It's almost like having a romantic liaison with someone you've never met before.

'Karen is more Mother's Day orientated than anybody, and I felt guilty about it. Before I told the boys about her, huge bunches of flowers would arrive from Interflora and cards that the postman couldn't get through the letterbox. I used to dread the postman coming. But Karen wanted to be noticed.

'I wish we could spend more time together. I fall in easily with her, but we haven't actually done a lot of talking. When she first rang me I was in shock, it hit me like a ton of bricks. Yet I knew it would happen — it's a funny feeling. This child seemed older than me and I was quite frightened by it. One of the first things she said was, "Why didn't you have an abortion?" and I thought to myself, yes, why didn't I? I didn't share it with anybody. I kept it to myself. One day I'd be OK, the next I'd be on the floor crying, and I had panic attacks.

'After Karen was adopted I hung on to the fact that the adoption society said they would send photographs. They didn't come and I thought maybe I shouldn't expect things. In the end I developed this non-excitement about everything; I was flat.

'I struggled all the time to keep a picture of the baby in my head. I did have a couple of photographs, and I hung on to them for years. Like a death, as the years went on the recurrent picture was fading. I was looking at little children as they progressed, and then I was thinking the people who have got her are giving her a good life. The adoption society assured me that they would look after her; obviously when you're bonded with a child you're very apprehensive about things like that. It's a hell of a thing to relinquish responsibility for a child.

'My second child was really a replacement for Karen. I just wanted to have something for myself. I felt that void for many years. I wouldn't say I could have snatched a baby, but I can understand the feelings women have and can't control.

'I've always done everything I've been told to do. I felt I had no rights at all. This affects my relationship with Karen now; I feel I have no right to reach out there because I rejected her. I signed the paper, and her life wasn't as I thought it would be. Nobody expects some idyllic fantasy, but you don't expect horror stories either.

'Karen used to phone me every three or four months. She never found anything out about me unless she asked me a question, but I listened. During one of the phone calls she was so abusive towards me, she thought I was the pits. I didn't have the experience of abusive teenagers I've since had with the boys. I took everything that came at me, and felt ill with guilt afterwards. It didn't occur to me not to. At the very end of the conversation, I said, "You've got a right to feel that way", and I still think that's true. The fact that I wasn't mentally old enough to handle it is irrelevant; she had a right to offload it.

'There's an underlying resentment which I still feel from her and I'm a bit nervous of it. But Karen finds it very difficult to let go, she hangs on to emotion.

'Another time she rang me in the middle of the night from a station. I nearly drove up to London. Somehow, out of my mouth came the words, "Where are you going?" as if it was quite normal to be on a station at one in the morning. That defused the situation. But I was still worried sick. I'm sure the adoptive mother was going through hell on earth. The rejection and everything is horrendous from your own children, never mind somebody else's, especially one that you've nurtured. I tried not to get too hooked emotionally. All I said to Karen was, "I will always be here at the other end of the telephone. I may not be able to come up with the goods, because I don't really know what you want from me. But certainly don't ever hesitate to ring here."

'When she rang and said she was pregnant I immediately said, are you happy? The next I heard she was getting married, and she phoned me three days before the wedding. I was still breastfeeding an 8-month-old baby myself, which she didn't know about. I thought my God, Karen will die if she knows there's another child. She said she wanted me to come to the wedding, and I said I can't. I thought, why can't I? She was crying, she was upset. I said it was the day for her and her husband, and that we shouldn't meet for the first time on that particular occasion. That must have been very hard for her; perhaps I'll talk to her about it some day.

'I felt awful on the day she was married; I almost felt tempted to get in the car and just go there, but I thought no, I must stick to my decision. I felt bad about the adoptive mother; there were lots of things I felt bad about and I didn't feel I had any right to be there. I think Karen was devastated in a way, although she seemed to accept it. But she cried, and I reacted to the crying. I felt blow it, let's get it over and done with, and I agreed to meet her the next day.

'I was a nervous wreck. When I met Karen I thought my God, she's just like me; it was like looking in a mirror. And out of all my children, she's the one that looks most like me, which made me feel guilty in a way. We both have this tension frown. And she's on edge in certain situations — I see it in myself and I recognise it in her.

'The picture of the baby that I had held for those years just evaporated. The emotions lasted for months afterwards; it doesn't just end that day. I dealt with it as best I could, but I felt inadequate. She asked me a lot about her father, as well as a lot of things I hadn't thought about, that were buried deep, so I found it quite difficult. Now she's clammed up; she doesn't ask at all. And I think there are some things she can't face up to herself — a bit like me. I understand how she feels, she doesn't want to rock the boat of her life. But I feel I've done everything she's wanted; she hasn't done anything I wanted. The balance is not right. I think this is the stumbling block, to be honest.

'Now that I've had experience with the boys, I feel I could get Karen to open up a bit, and feel that I've got the right to do that. Whereas before I've been very good, because otherwise she might not like me — I was anxious to please, to say the right thing.'

Karen, too, has always been anxious to say the right thing. The need to be on best behaviour sets them apart from other mothers and daughters, who are more likely to be on their worst behaviour much of the time, with neither side necessarily taking umbrage. Like many adopted women Karen's curiosity about her birth mother grew out of a general desire to find out about her background.

Karen had an unhappy life with her adoptive family; her parents had a pretty rocky marriage, and Karen's adoptive father, whom she adored, died when she was a young child. Karen admits, 'I think I must have been a difficult teenager because I was quite an angry sort of person.' She started to ring Gill during those difficult teenage years, when she was rejecting her adoptive mother out of hand. It's surely no coincidence that soon after she made contact with Gill, she found the confidence to leave home.

'I started to think about looking for my mother when I was about 12. At first the need to know something about my background used to nag away at the back of my mind, but then it was really my mum that I was interested in.

'A lot of adopted people I've talked to fantasise about their mother — that it's someone famous, the usual fantasies — but I didn't have any picture of what she would look like or be like. When you don't know anyone who's like you, you don't know what to expect really. It's a wicked thing to say, but in the back of my mind I really hoped that she wasn't the dregs of the earth.

'When I met her it was like seeing a double vision; she's so like me. It was very strange, because obviously I'd never met anyone who looked remotely like me before. I was surprised how alike we are; it's unreal, considering she didn't bring me up. When I look at her other children I think I'm the only one who looks like her — and we have similar views on things.

'I don't really think of either of them as mum. I haven't spoken to my adoptive mother since just after my son was born. I used to go round for afternoon tea, and do the usual bit, but it was just as bad as it was when I was living there. Finally I said I didn't want any more to do with her. I know it sounds cold, but it was a decision I didn't take lightly. Her first reaction was, what am I supposed to tell everybody, that you're dead? I think her ego took a bashing more than anything. She was hurt, but then I'd been hurt for sixteen years.

'My adoptive parents didn't have a good marriage; I think they adopted me hoping it might make their relationship better. My mother had an affair on and off, and in the end she got pregnant with my younger sister. Everybody pretended the baby was my father's. Then he died. I found out later that the plan was for my mother and her boyfriend to go off with my sister and be the happy family, and for me to live with my adoptive dad, but things didn't work out like that, and so I was resented, I suppose. Even as a child you're aware of that kind of friction.

'There was constant tension and battles between my parents. After my father died, my mother's boyfriend didn't come and live with us, but he would just let himself in when she wasn't there. I was always miserable; it took me a long time to sort myself out, and the only way I was going to do it was to put all that behind me. I feel a lot better having done it.

'I tend to have a cut-off point between the old and the new life. The cut-off point was when I left home when I was 16. It was dramatic stuff; I just took the basics. I left after an argument with my mother's boyfriend after he'd been drinking. When I went back three days later it was as if it had never happened; my mother didn't even mention it. So I left for good.

'When I was 16 and I'd decided I was going to leave home anyway, because things had got so bad, I was at a friend's house one day and I decided to phone my birth mother. I got the number from directory enquiries; my adoptive mother had told me my real name and my birth mother's name, which was quite an unusual one, and where she lived. Directory enquiries gave me five numbers and the third one I tried was my mum's brother, and he gave me the number. I told him I was an old school friend of hers. Looking back it was completely the wrong way to go about it, but at the time it was just an impulse — my friend and I were messing about and it seemed like a good idea at the time. When I phoned my mother she answered, and she knew who it was as soon as I spoke; she had this feeling that it was me. There was a dead silence at the other end; she was quite upset. After the initial shock we were on the phone for over two hours — it was what do you look like and the basic information and so on.

'A couple of months after that I left home. I used to phone Gill every couple of months. I didn't know what I was phoning her for — at that stage, when you haven't met the person, it's just chit-chat.

'We had a few years' phone contact before the first meeting. When I was pregnant, we decided to get married, so I rang Gill to tell her. We decided on the phone that it wouldn't be a good idea if she came to the wedding, because of emotions running high and so on, so I met her at my sister-in-law's house the Friday before.

'I didn't want to push the meeting; I felt I'd infringed anyway, because I'd just gone in like a bull in a china shop and said hello, here I am, with no consideration to her whatsoever. Everyone used to say, don't you want to meet her, but I felt, if she wants to see me, we'll go from there. At least I knew where she was; we'd made contact.

'Before I met her she rang up and said, "Before I come up and see you, there's something I've got to tell you." She had an 8-month baby daughter, who she had never mentioned before. There was communication between us, but it was really just on the surface, it was a farce really.

At the time that didn't bother me; it was neither here nor there. I already knew about my two half-brothers. I've never asked her why she hadn't told me about the baby; I can't see any reason to withhold it. Her daughter is 5 now; she's just a year older than my son, which I find quite weird. It's difficult to think of her as my half-sister.

'When Gill and I first met it was all very polite. Now we're more open with each other and we get on better. We see each other every few months. Because I've got my own life, which is quite full, and my family, I don't have time to resent the fact that she gave me up, but not the others. I do sometimes wish she hadn't given me up, but you can't turn the clock back. You've just got to be thankful for what you've got — I mean, I might never have found her, that's the way I look at it. Some people who search for their birth mothers find that they're dead, which must be awful. If she'd rejected me I don't know how I would have coped. The reason I didn't phone her very much at the beginning was because it was always there in the back of my mind that any minute she could say, "I've had enough, I don't want to know."'

The way Karen made contact with Gill is exceptional. Most adopted women who try to find their birth mothers face a series of obstacles, both emotional and practical. Tracking down a parent is rarely easy; what can be most difficult to handle is the idea that, having been rejected once, you might be in for another rejection. But as Karen and Gill discovered, the problems certainly don't end with the first meeting.

One of the biggest nightmares must be reconciling the two images of the mother; the chances are that, like Susan's two mothers, they will be poles apart. Susan, who is 29 and met her birth mother for the first time just over a year ago, says, 'If my birth mother and my adoptive mother met each other without any connection, they would hate each other. They're just completely different women.' She describes her birth mother as a scatty, crazy woman who enjoys a risqué joke, and her adoptive mother as much more strait-laced: very efficient and very moral.

Susan's recognition of what she perceived to be the difference between a birth mother's love and an adoptive mother's love hit her with full force when her first daughter was born. It was a shattering experience which led to clinical depression. Like Karen, meeting the birth mother with whom she feels such a natural affinity has convinced her that the blood tie is all important.

Susan has to keep reassuring her adoptive mother that her relationship with her birth mother doesn't threaten her love for her. But at the same time she feels a much more immediate sympathy and rapport with her birth mother. As she says, it's a minefield of conflicting emotions. Susan's story is peppered so frequently with declarations of love for her adoptive mother, that you can't help but feel that she protests too much, for she also makes some pretty damning remarks about her mother's unrealistic expectations. It's not surprising that Susan feels ambivalent: she genuinely loves her adoptive mother, but can't help blaming her for the way she was brought up to feel 'second best'. At the same time she feels guilty about criticising her mother, and unhappy that finding her birth mother has caused so much pain. Yet Susan's ambivalence about both her mothers contrasts sharply with her clearcut views on how she plans to bring up her own daughters.

There is also a hint of disappointment with her birth mother, who she also 'loves to pieces'; she can't rid herself of the feeling that nothing could have induced her to give up a baby. She's been hurt by her mother's forgetfulness, although she dismisses it as scattiness, one of the qualities she most identifies with. Similarly, the fact that 'she never makes the effort to come down' seems to jar. But for Susan, it's early days: she met her mother just over a year ago, and one suspects that the initial excitement has yet to die down. When it has, there will still be a minefield of emotions to explore.

Both Susan and Karen identify closely with their birth mothers: perhaps because, as Susan says, before they met she felt like a leaf without a branch. Both women stress how closely they resemble their birth mothers, in both looks and personality. And for both, the initial contact with the birth mother was followed by an increase in self-esteem. Susan started selling her paintings and singing in public, while Karen, 16 at the time, found the confidence to leave home. It's as if having found someone else to rely on she could afford to cut herself off from the adoptive mother whom she felt so hard done by.

Susan was prompted to look for her mother by the birth of her own daughter, Ruth: 'It suddenly brought home to me the difference between the love for a natural child and for an adopted child. It hit me very hard. I could immediately see the difference in the way my adoptive parents loved me and the way I loved my daughter; it was completely different. Even as a baby, I accepted that she was who she was; I loved her regardless of what she was. But with mum and dad, I suppose they'd spent so many years wanting a child, that by the time they got round to adopting me, they had in their minds the great plan of what I was going to do, what I was going to be like, right down to where I was going to be educated, how I was going to dress even — everything. And of course, I didn't fit, because I wasn't their child. We love each other to pieces, but we don't understand each other at all. It hurts a lot, an awful lot.

'I went through a long period of being very depressed, and of hating my birth mother as well. I couldn't imagine any circumstances under which I would part with my baby. I tried to rationalise it by saying it was twenty-five years ago, and so on. Eventually I realised there must have been mitigating circumstances, I came to terms with it and I stopped hating her for it. That's when I needed to look; before I'd just been a little bit curious.

'I used to think about my birth mother on every birthday, and sometimes in between; I used to wonder if she was thinking about me. I always imagined her as a very tall, very beautiful woman who was very kind and very loving and who had to give me up because it was life or death. And as someone who thought about me all the time and was longing to see me. When the social workers

117

warned me that she might not want to see me I thought, "I'm her daughter, so she must be like me in some ways, and I know how I'd feel if I'd had a child adopted. I'd want them to contact me at some point; I'd want to know she was OK."

'For a couple of years after I had my daughter I was very badly depressed, to the extent that I wouldn't get washed or dressed, I wouldn't cook. I would see to Ruth when she needed it; she was immaculate and always well fed and everything. But I was in a daze. In the end the health visitor sent me to a psychiatrist. I'm sure an element of it was post-natal depression, but the majority of it was this adoption thing — it was such a shock to me. The rosy picture suddenly popped and there I was in the real world. It was nightmarish.

'I never thought about finding my father, not once. It was purely a maternal thing, because there's not another love like your love for your kids; it transcends everything. You might say, "I'd die for you" to a boyfriend but you know that when the crunch came you wouldn't. But with your kids you wouldn't hesitate — that's the difference. It was the strength of emotion I felt for my daughters opposed to what I saw as the lack of emotion my birth mother must have felt for me that made me look for her. I felt dreadfully rejected then.

'That's when the trips up to the adoption society started. Then I discovered I had a full sister who was older than me, and that started the hatred off again. I just couldn't fathom out why she kept my sister and not me. It was a long hard trail, it was just soul-destroying and frustrating and, in the end, after about five years I gave up. A friend took it over without me knowing.

'I got a telephone call from this friend one Friday morning saying, "What are you doing, can I pop down and see you? I've got someone I'd like you to meet." I said OK. I was standing in the kitchen and I looked up and saw this woman walking past the window and it was just electric, I knew it was my sister the second I laid eyes on her. We flew into each other's arms; it was like something out of the movies. When I'd calmed down, she told me my mum was in the car and I nearly fell through the floor. It was probably the best thing, to be totally unprepared like that, otherwise I would have got into a complete state. I stood in the kitchen looking at my mother and my head started buzzing and I felt so faint. We just stood and stared at each other open mouthed.

'They stayed the weekend, and I don't think I've ever laughed or cried so much. It was an amazing experience. Suddenly I was home; I was with people I fitted with. We talked about absolutely everything. It was wonderful. I was exactly like them, from the largest things down to the tiniest little things. For example, we did our make up identically — we use the same brand and the same colours. I look like my mother. My mother's character and my character are virtually identical. The only difference is that there's a hard streak in her that I haven't got, thank goodness. But then I've had an easy life compared to them — my mother's been married four times.

'When my sister was about 18 months old, my mother found out that the father was playing around and left him. She then discovered she was pregnant with me. Her mother and father didn't approve of her having my sister because she was out of wedlock and the thought of another baby was just too much so she decided to give me up for adoption. I can understand the pressure she must have been under, but I think it's a real shame. Having had two children myself I know that it's not that much harder. I'm separated, I'm on my own with the kids and I haven't got any money and life's a real struggle, but you manage. I've never said it to her, but in the back of my mind and in my heart there's the thought, you could have tried, mum. The other thing that really hurt me, and again I haven't told her because she's a very sensitive lady, was when I asked her about a letter which the adoption society had told me she had written when I was about 6 months old, to find out how I was. She said, "Oh, no, dear, I didn't do that. As soon as I'd given you up for adoption I even forgot which society you were with." I was horrified — you don't forget which society you've put your baby with, for God's sake. She said you know what my memory's like, and that she was very stressed. So I have to give her the benefit of the doubt. But it's such a minefield of emotion.

'Before I felt like a leaf with no branch to hang on to and now suddenly I fit, I can see why my adoptive parents and I had so many ups and downs. I always felt it was my fault, that there was something basically wrong with me that I was letting them down so often. But at the same time, being a bit of a rebel, I wouldn't sacrifice my principles. Now I can see where I get it from, and I can see that if I'd lived there, I'd never have felt that. So it was circumstance rather than me that was at fault. Discovering this increased my self-esteem a lot.

'In retrospect I was just a normal teenager, but because there's such a difference between my parents and me I was made to feel it was my fault. I thought they must be right; you get sort of brainwashed into thinking that. They had the best intentions, but they had this great master plan, and for them to admit that it was perhaps fallible would have meant that the whole structure of their lives would have crumbled. They had to hang on to it because it was all they'd got. They were forever trying to mould me into it; they still do, even now.

'My adoptive mother is a very efficient, very career-minded, very Victorian morals type woman — a lovely lady. I'm scatty and untidy and totally disorganised. My parents wanted me to get a degree and have a career; I never wanted that; I wanted to paint. They said you're good but you'll never make a living out of it.

'I found out about periods in sex education at school. When I asked mum about it she said it's something that we don't talk about. I remember when I was 13 asking my mum what having intercourse was like — I'd just learned this big word at school. She said, "Yes well, it's something that's over very quickly and it's very messy and it's just something you have to do if you want children." I never asked her at all after that because she obviously didn't want to talk about it at all; it really embarrassed her, bless her heart.

'I was pregnant when I got married, which absolutely horrified them. On my wedding morning my mother said, "Your father wanted to be proud of you when he walked down the aisle, and this is what you've done to him." It was awful. Now I'm selling my paintings and I sing which they poopooed at. They heard me in a concert recently and they said my God you really can sing. They never listen to what I say because they don't have any respect for me. They're right and I'm not, which is very sad and very frustrating.

'I was determined that come hell or high water my daughter was going to be the happiest child I could possibly make her. She was going to grow up secure and happy. I've failed abysmally, because my husband and I have separated. When it first happened I was very upset because I felt I was on the same road as my birth mother, and I had to pull myself up sharp and recognise that it was just a mistake.

'I was determined that Ruth would always feel loved and wanted, no matter what she does. She could become a prostitute, God forbid, and I might not like her very much, but I would always love her to pieces.

'I wanted daughters. I can relate to little girls much better than I can to little boys. I suppose that's got something to do with being adopted as well. The need for that feminine, maternal thing is very strong in me. I always feel that I've got to compensate for feeling the way that I always did; it's like a knot in my stomach all the time; my daughters have got to know that they're safe with me.

'It was a year ago in March that my mother and I met. She doesn't make the effort to come down; I've been to stay the weekend with her seven or eight times now. When we see each other, we fly into each other's arms; it's a great bond between us. There are parts of her that I don't like at all, but I love her to pieces. Our likes and dislikes are very similar, but our attitudes and morals are different. I suppose that's due to the way I was brought up. There's a gulf between us, and sometimes it comes out very strongly. But we get on like a house on fire; I can talk about anything with my mother; she's absolutely crazy.

'I always wished that my adoptive mother would look at me as a person and not as an image she'd got of me. I felt that the mother I found was the kind of mother I had always wanted. I suddenly thought this is how it should be, because that's what I'm like. She's me; I'm her. Having said that, I do feel that my adoptive mother is my mum, because she brought me up. It's like living two separate existences. I love my birth mother very much and she is my mother; but she's not my mum. There's a big difference.

'Unfortunately I'm having a lot of difficulty getting that across to my mum and dad. They're very hurt. They can't accept it at all. I hate to see them hurt. They keep expecting me to uproot and go and live near my birth mother. I was shaking when I went round to tell them that I was looking for my natural mother. At that point they were amazing. They said they thought the time would come that I would have to do this. They even offered to help. But as soon as I found my mother it was a different matter. It didn't help that my adopted brother is violently opposed to anyone suggesting that he's adopted. He didn't talk to me for over a year because of what I did. Yet again I was the black sheep of the family. He conforms; he gets on with them. They see my questioning as a rejection of them.

'I don't feel jealous of my sister, but I do feel resentful when they take out the photo albums and there's mum and my sister and my half-brother (he was born two years after she gave me up for adoption; that really hurt) on the beach and at the amusement park and I think I should have been there. The knife turns a bit. But my sister's just as much a victim as me.

'When I was pregnant my adoptive mother couldn't relate to me at all. I wanted to involve her in the pregnancy, but when I offered to let her feel the baby kick she didn't really want to. In retrospect, trying to involve her might have been a mistake, but I felt it was almost like, here, I'm giving you this child, I'm bearing this child so you can share it.

'The other thing was that I threw up constantly — my mother was the same apparently. My adoptive mother used to tell me to pull myself together, she'd say, you're not ill, you're pregnant. And I thought, there speaks a woman who hasn't had a child. The whole thing was embarrassing, it was as if I had to pretend that I wasn't pregnant. That made me miss my mother. I needed somebody to talk to about how I was feeling — the fears you always get when you're pregnant, and about being so ill too. I wanted someone to understand. But I think my mother coped admirably under the circumstances, because it must have hurt every time she looked at me. The injustice of it makes my heart bleed for her.

'There were just two occasions when she let her feelings come through. The first was when I was breastfeeding Ruth and as she unlatched from one breast the milk came out in sprays. She said, "My God, I never thought it came out like that." She was absolutely astounded, but a few seconds later she'd pulled herself together and she was detached again. The only other time was directly after I had Ruth, who was very ill after she was born. My parents were allowed to see her out of the incubator for a few seconds and my mum went, "Oh my God!" at all the emotion that was there, she absolutely adored her.

'She was wonderful when the babies were born. And when they hit 6 weeks something happened to her, I could see it in her face. She said, "This is the age we had you from"; it was like from now on in I can relate to this, I'm at home with this now. She's a wonderful grandmother; she's far more patient with them than she was with me, but I suppose that's true of all grandparents.

'I'm already bringing my daughters up very differently to the way I was brought up. My mother dressed me until I was 9. My daughters are so much more independent than I was; my mother wanted to look after me, to do everything for me. I want them to be their own people, even now. I don't want them ever to feel they ought to be something they're not. I let them develop their own characters as much as I possibly can. I don't want them to have the hang-ups I had, though having said that, they'll probably have a whole different set of hang-ups. I never want them to feel they've got to do something because I want them to do it. If I was ever told to do something, my instinct was to rebel. So I reason with the girls. That's the complete antithesis to the way I was brought up and they're very strong, independent children because of it.

'I want them to know that they can come to me with anything, just as I feel I can go to my birth mother with anything. I think that will happen, because of the sort of people that they are and the sort of person that I am. We are friends now — although I know it's different with kids than when they're grown up. I want them to think of me as one of the buddies, and I'm sure they will because my attitude is the same as my birth mother's. It might all backfire, but so be it. I don't want them to be under any emotional blackmail at all.

'You can't make a general statement about how important the blood tie is, because I know people who've lived with their natural parents all their lives and get on much worse than I do with my adoptive parents. But in my experience the blood tie is very important — when you haven't known who your mother is, you just don't know who you are, you have no identity to relate to — the blood tie is absolutely crucial. It's such an unnerving feeling. I was reading a book which said it was very rare that a man wanted to know who his natural mother was — all the people who had come forward to be interviewed were women, and they felt that they just had to know. I think that the maternal bond is such that you can't get away from it. It's too strong.'

Yet some women who have been abandoned by their mothers as children, like Heather, now in her early forties, feel that the maternal bond has been severed for good by that early rejection. Heather refuses to give her mother, who now lives nearby, much thought; she certainly makes no attempt to understand her because she feels what she did was unforgivable.

'My mother left us when I was 6. My granny in Wilt-shire looked after us until I was 10, then I came to Derby to live with my dad and my stepmother, who really was a bitch. My mum lives at Derby now, but I don't get on with her. I haven't got any time for her because she didn't want us when we were little. I can't understand any woman leaving her kids, although I can understand a man doing the same. I don't see her unless I can help it.'

Heather's uncompromising view is understandable. Diane, who abandoned a daughter twenty-five years ago, thinks that there can be good reasons for leaving a child, though in retrospect she thinks her own reason wasn't good enough. When Diane, a 50-year-old American, left her first husband she also left her eldest daughter, Monique, then 2, to be brought up by an aunt. Not long afterwards she came to Great Britain, where she now lives with her two younger daughters, Sarah and Vicky. Diane's decision, which she says was taken so lightly at the time, changed her life.

Recently, the tightly stretched bond between mother and daughter was strengthened by the unwitting inter-vention of Diane's youngest daughter Sarah.

'I never denied that this child existed and that she was Vicky and Sarah's sister, but living so far away from each other there wasn't a lot of relationship until we were there one summer and Sarah and Monique were both in their teens. You could see they liked each other; there was a lot of gossip and so on. They began to write to one another. I hadn't had a lot of contact with Monique, but through these letters I became closer to the daughter that I no longer saw and there was an acknowledgement of mother and child, an acknowledgement of two sisters. Sarah started talking about her sister who lived in America; it all became quite open. I was pleased and I was fascinated how a child could improve the relationship between a mother and another daughter.

'I abandoned Monique to marry Sarah and Vicky's father. She was brought up by her aunt as her daughter; she called her mom. She calls me mom too; she knows I'm her mother and she realises the blood ties.

'At the time I don't think I knew what I was doing. I was very immature and I wanted what I wanted. I wanted that sweetie in that shop window and I had no regard for anyone or anything. I couldn't do it again. I can see that child to this day, I can see her the last time I saw her — I know what she was wearing, it was snowing, she was standing at a bus stop with her auntie. It's a painful memory. I would never do that to a child again, although I understand women who do it for different reasons. I've worked with children — disturbed adolescents and very young children — for many years and a lot that goes into that work is the knowledge that children can be very, very hurt by the treatment of their parents. I think that part of the reason I work with children is that I did this to one child myself, and I was going to protect other children from hurt as much as I possibly could without becoming their parent.

'I couldn't see Monique that often because we moved to the UK when Vicky was 10 months old, but any opportunity I had to go to the US I saw her. It was always arranged that we would spend time together, but it became more so as she grew older and we had more things that we could do together.

'In the beginning my mother and the rest of my family were very disapproving. In the end I made it up with my parents. My dad once said to me, "Never ever come over here without your children." It was sort of a warning, that you've done that to one child, you're never to leave any of your children anywhere, you're to keep them with you. So when my second marriage temporarily broke down, I had very confused feelings about Vicky [then a teenager] staying with her dad, even though we weren't far from one another. I held Sarah very close to me indeed. I wasn't ever giving up any children again.

'I think Monique speculates about why I abandoned her. Outwardly she doesn't seem resentful, but I don't know. I would like to discuss it with her and I've come close to it. I feel the time will come.'

Helen's separation from her teenage daughter, which began when she was 8, brings its own particular anxieties. She worries constantly about the lack of female guidance, advice and sympathy a teenage girl so badly needs. The separation hasn't been continuous; Claudia lived with Helen, and with her English grandmother, for a couple of years before returning to her father in Italy three years ago. Helen's mother, Peggy, gives a poignant account of the first reunion between mother and daughter: 'When we went over to Italy with Helen to collect Claudia, poor Claudia just sat and gazed at her mother, she just looked and looked at her. When she came to England she was in a very bad state in that she couldn't bear Helen to be out of sight and eventually, because Helen was working, she got used to being associated with me, but she wouldn't go to anybody else. One of Helen's friends in Italy told me that after Helen left them Claudia couldn't bear to be out of sight of people — if she went to the loo she'd leave the door open so that she could see that everybody was still there.

'I can remember Helen ringing from a bar at the beach and saying she just wanted to hear a voice. The next thing was this phone call from her husband saying he'd put Helen on the train. I said, "And the children?" and he said, "No, the children are staying here." I can't bear to think of it even now, they were so close to their mother, and to have her taken from them like that must have been dreadful.'

In spite of the separation, mother and daughter get on well when Claudia visits during the school holidays. However, her mother is concerned about the absence of any female influence in the Italian household. 'What worries me is the lack of guidance, and I think she probably feels that too. Having to cope with periods on her own, coping with growing up, I get upset that I'm not there to help her cope with that sort of thing; she's only young, after all. And I don't know who she's got to talk about boyfriends to — it must be rather lonely.'

9.
ROLE REVERSAL

'She would imagine that I was trying to kill her. It still harks back to the days when it was the most dreadful thing in the world if your mother shouted at you and it would still get me in that way. It's very hard to act in a logical way.'

Jane

'I felt torn apart between my responsibilities for my kids and what my mother and all her relations seemed to see as my responsibilities to her.'

Maeve

Most women, no matter what their age, rely on their mothers for some kind of support. It's a pattern of one-way nurture established early in life, which often continues long into adulthood, for better or worse.

So what happens when a mother needs support herself, either practical help, because of illness or age, or emotional support, when she's going through some sort of crisis — a divorce, say, or a breakdown or bereavement? It is still usually the daughter — rarely the son — who is expected to step in to offer the kind of back-up she may have always taken for granted from her mother.

Unfair though it may seem, it's not hard to see why the burden of caring and support rests on daughters rather than sons. Daughters tend to be better at it — not only are they made in their mother's image, they're also likely to have more experience of the caring role with their own children. And they're available: however pressing their domestic commitments, these can be accommodated in a way that the male breadwinner's cannot. Or at least that's how it appears to the outside world.

Daughters tend to be better at emotional support too.

Often a daughter can provide the kind of comfort which no one else can; she knows the situation and the personalities involved better than anyone else, without having to be told. Some problems are too painful, or too personal, to discuss with a friend, let alone a stranger.

But how easy is it for daughters, accustomed as they are to seeing their mothers as nurturers, to step into the supportive role? And how can they stop it getting out of hand, without hurting feelings? Some mothers still think it's their daughter's duty to care for them in their dotage, while others simply get used to their daughter's attentions and don't want them to stop or even ease up. So for many women there comes a point when they have to distance themselves before their mother's emotional dependence becomes too great, particularly if they've got children and careers themselves. Yet society does not expect daughters to maintain a distance; nor do many mothers, fiercely backed up by relatives and friends.

Yet the women I spoke to all felt that there was a positive side to the reversal of roles, however painful the experience. They all felt that in some way, their mother's illness, or the crisis they had survived together, had brought them closer. Some found that, perhaps because the usual routes of communication had been truncated, they were able to be much more physically demonstrative than they had been in the past; showing affection in a very direct way took on a new importance.

Most of us keep our fingers firmly crossed that our mothers won't become disabled or too dependent with old age, and that we will never have to face the dread prospect of putting mother in a home. With the elderly population on the increase, it's a problem more and more women are likely to face. Yet caring for the elderly, like caring for children, is given short shrift in our society; the fact that millions of people devote their lives to caring for relatives goes virtually unrecognised. At least looking after children has a brighter image — even nappies and buggies get portrayed with a certain amount of glamour by the advertising industry — but we've yet to see incontinence pads and wheelchairs given the same kind of treatment.

But old age and disability don't necessarily go hand in hand; illness can strike at any age. Jane and her mother have been unlucky; Jane's mother started to suffer from Alzheimer's disease eighteen years ago, when Jane was in her mid-twenties and her mother was in her late fifties. Jane resisted institutionalised care until she finally reached the stage when she felt she could no longer cope, five years ago. Jane is an only child, and her parents separated when she was 2, so she's the only person available to care for her mother.

Like many women in her position, it took her a long time — years in her case — to face up to the reality of the situation. She looks back on the period since her mother first became ill with some guilt, many regrets for the close relationship they once had, and great sadness. Here she describes her mother's unusually gradual deterioration.

'My mother started to suffer from Alzheimer's disease about the time her second marriage broke up. We were living together in Australia at the time. I noticed things like she would check her bag about six times. She was very emotional — smashing a vase would upset her terribly. It was a very upsetting time anyway; the breakdown of the marriage was a great upheaval.

'We moved from Adelaide to Sydney and she couldn't really handle the jobs that she got there. In many ways it would have been better if we had just stayed put and she had had a long stretch of the same pattern. But at that stage I didn't know what was wrong with her, I just thought it was a long emotional period of readjusting and change of life and not being able to cope and so on. And in a way I suppose there was a sort of unwillingness in me to admit that there was anything major wrong, other than something she could snap out of and then get on with her life.

'Then we came back to England and she lived with various relatives, which didn't work out well, so mum got a flat in Colchester, which is where we used to live, and I lived in London. All this time I was living my life and not accepting the responsibility. Then one day I got a phone call at work. Mum was very worried because she had just laid out two lots of cups and saucers and she had made a cup of tea for my Auntie Emily, who had been dead for thirty-odd years.

'So she came up to London to stay with me; I was living in a house with other girls in Putney. After a while she went back to Colchester, but it was obvious when I went down for weekends that she just wasn't managing. The girls in my house said I could have her to live there, and I had a big room, so she came up and lived with us. It was a pretty disastrous move because they were quite nice girls, but very English middle-class and they just didn't accept that she was very peculiar; she couldn't tell the time and she would leave things in funny places in the kitchen. People would ring up and she would give peculiar answers because she was very frustrated at being there. It was all nightmarish; to have put her through that was just dreadful. She always felt a nuisance, she always felt in the way. As soon as any of the girls came back, she would beetle up to our room and hide herself. This more aggressive side of her nature would come out and she would get very angry, so that would come out in other ways, like answering the phone and being rude to everybody.

'I still didn't know what was the matter with her and I think probably part of my nature is not to face up to things, to pretend that they aren't happening, or that they'll go away. She did go to doctors but she never told the full story; she would go and say, "I'm having lots of headaches," and he would say, "Never mind, dear, it's your age." Then she went to a woman doctor who gave all her new patients a thorough examination, and she noticed that mum got in a muddle as she got undressed. She sent mum for all sorts of tests.

'At the time we were trying to decide whether to go back to Australia, and I rang the hospital to ask if mum was fit enough to travel in the near future. The doctor said no, and I also asked if he had the results of the tests. He said, "Oh yes, Mrs Jarvis, she's dementing, isn't she?" Now I had never heard this word in relation to anybody I knew, it was a sort of joke word and it really got me. That was facing the thing, I suppose, it was shoved right in my face. I expected to go home and find mum running round the house tearing her hair out or something so it was a relief to find her relatively normal.

'So then I had an idea of what was going to happen, although it was fairly vague because she could deteriorate rapidly, or she could reach a plateau and stay there for a long time. The situation in the house was getting impossible, and an aunt who lived in Norfolk suggested mum bought a house near her and offered to look after her. She didn't realise how ill mum was. So again, I saw this as a way out, not in so many words, but that's what it was.

'For a while it worked very well and I used to go up every third weekend, then every other weekend. There would be a lot of clearing up and sorting out to do every time. Then my aunt and my mother fell out, and my aunt came back to live in London. Mum was left on her own up there, so I had to go up every weekend. I would get phone calls from the police saying she had been arrested for shoplifting and then I got reports that she was walking around the town without trousers on. Again, it probably would have been better if I had moved up there, but I wasn't prepared to give up what I had down here, like friends and the sort of things that I did. So mum moved into a flat I was renting in Hampstead, and we stayed there for five years. By this time she couldn't really go out; if she did she couldn't find her way back, and so the whole pattern shifted. At one stage I was having to dash home at lunchtime to give her lunch and then dash home in the evening to give her a meal and an outing. All the day she just had to sit up there on her own, there was nothing she could do except listen to the radio.

'She started going to a day centre three days a week, which was a bit traumatic. Even at that stage (she was in her late sixties) she looked really sophisticated, and to see her get into this Camden van, looking so worried and forlorn, was awful. Occasionally she would refuse to go and that would cause all sorts of problems because I'd have to come home at lunchtime, then pedal home furiously in the evening not knowing what I was going to find. She didn't as a rule turn on things like the gas, she was more likely to tear things apart. She was also doubly incontinent, that was the major thing really.

'All this time we kept a basis of friendship and in a way I became closer to her then, because although we had been very close before, we had not been terribly demonstrative, we'd never hugged or kissed, or said I love you, which was now the only way, more or less, I could communicate with her.

'About halfway through this five-year period she started to have hallucinations, which was a very large fly in the ointment. She would imagine that I was saying all sorts of things about her, that I was trying to kill her. The peculiar thing about it is that it still harks back to the days when it was the most dreadful thing in the world if your mother shouted at you and it would still get me in that way. It's very hard to act in a logical way about it, to bear in mind that she's not responsible for what she's saying. She's still your mother shouting at you and accusing you of trying to kill her when all you're trying to do is make life bearable for her.

'I learned that you don't argue about it, if she says something is one way, then you go along with it. You don't say don't be stupid, because it just escalates. Once we even came to blows and I thought that if I went hysterical it would somehow stop her, but it didn't. What you have to do is just keep your voice on a very even level. You have to keep your own emotions in check and then it will cool down, which is very hard. It got pretty ghastly; I remember one morning she pulled the curtain off the rail and threw a cup of tea at me in her rage.

'I occasionally used to go away for residential weekends with this philosophy school I belong to; I'd start planning about a month in advance. I never felt guilty because I wasn't going to lie on a beach all weekend, I was just going to improve myself. The thing I did feel guilty about was leaving her in a home for a week when I was on holiday.

The place was completely wrong, and when I picked her up she was so relieved to see me, and not cross at all. I did feel guilty about it, but I sort of stuffed that under the carpet. The other thing was, it was extremely hard to come back after a week off and take it up again.

'Anyway we soldiered on for five years and then mum started falling over and she couldn't get up unless there was someone there to help her. So that was the catalyst for the next move.

'I found what I thought was a lovely private home, close enough so I could spend lots of time there. My great mistake was that I didn't actually take her there, and I didn't talk to mum about it because she would forget the next day, so I waited for the day to dawn to introduce the idea. I took her up there and she walked in the door and said, "I know what sort of place this is." She hadn't spoken in sentences for ages and suddenly she gathered all her strength and said, "You've no right to bring me here, I'm not staying," and she was absolutely dreadful. In my brain I was so certain it was the answer to everything and suddenly it was all shot down, I was devastated.

'I was going on holiday a couple of months later so I arranged with the social worker that she would take her to a home in south London and she went without a murmur. When a place became available in Hampstead she went there, but she couldn't feed herself, she couldn't do anything, so they couldn't keep her. So after about nine months the proposition was put to me that she had to go into hospital. I had always thought I couldn't possibly allow her to do that, but having been relieved for nine months I felt I couldn't possibly take it up again.

'I drove her up to the hospital and it was awful. I decided to switch off and do it. She cried as we drove along, but she had deteriorated to such a stage that you didn't know whether it was related to what was actually going on, or to some sort of fantasy she was having.

'She's been there now for about five years. To begin with I used to cry for the first fifteen minutes every time I went, and I didn't think anybody was noticing. Then one of the nurses tried to jolly me out of it one day and I just was not in the mood and I told her to go away and leave me alone. She got terribly upset and reported it, and the clinical psychologist called me in and decided I was a suitable case for treatment.

'It did wake me up to the fact that people do notice and I talked to somebody about it who said that really you have to accept the fact that she's gone, she just isn't there any more, and that made it a lot easier. All the tears were about how it should be, how it was, has it come to this? It was all harking back to the past. So from then on it was much better, I didn't cry any more, or just occasionally. She has gone, but then there's this person who occasionally reminds you incredibly, by some little movement or expression. I don't think she recognises me any more, sometimes it comes through but there's not a lot of response.

'One thing that is very peculiar is that it's very difficult to remember what she was really like, because she's been so strange for so long, and my most vivid memories of her are as she has been in the last ten years or so. We were always very comfortable together and as time went by she would always do what I wanted her to do; wherever I wanted to go, she would just come along. I've never found this in any other relationship.

'I remember the last proper conversation we had was in Norfolk and she was worried that I wasn't enjoying life as I should. She thought I should be doing different things and I was trying to convince her that I was perfectly happy with the life I was living.

'Up until her illness I had always moved around a lot, but when I came back to England I felt that I wanted to stay in one place for a while, and I wasn't able to do anything else looking after her, so the two coincided. Now I've got into a bit of a rut where I find it difficult to do anything else, and in any case I still find that having her there is a tie. I get five weeks' leave at the end of this year, and I was going to go to Australia, but I think twice about it. I don't know if I could leave her for that long without anybody. Whether she knows me or not I don't know, but I would feel bad about leaving her for that long without anybody to go in and be special to her.

'I used to turn down lots of invitations, because with this philosophy school I was out two or three nights a week anyway, and I always felt that extra outings were not really justified. I felt OK with that because I felt I ought to be doing it, but I didn't feel OK about going to parties and things. I used to have people round a lot more than I do now. It's funny that, because she was there and I was looking after her it somehow made it a home and a family in a way, so I tended to invite people round a lot more. The people who came knew about her and were willing to accept the situation.

'When I stopped living with her I didn't have a role any more; I didn't have a purpose for a while. This flat was always less of a home because she's not here, and I don't like living alone, it brings out the worst in me. I just flop in front of the television; I got a lot more done when I was looking after her than I do now.

'I did feel resentful in the beginning. I remember when this man talked about dementia, I felt this great wave of resentment that I was going to have to spend the rest of my life — or an awfully long time — pitching my life to this 60-odd-year-old demented woman. I felt very angry for a while, but it did go. It's like you think you can't possibly drive through London, but you're sitting in the middle of the traffic and you just have to do it. So when you're in the situation you just have to cope with it.'

The new closeness which Jane describes — in her case a physical intimacy she had never experienced with her mother before — seems to be an integral part of dependence; it's almost like a silver lining to the cloud of any period of crisis. Pippa has always had a difficult relationship with her mother, who she describes as a strong, domineering woman. 'We were in different worlds,' she remembers. But then her father's death, and her mother's illness (she suffers from Parkinson's disease) forged a bond between them. Pippa, who is 29 and has three sons, and her elder sister are committed to the idea that their mother won't go into a home; the plan is that when her condition deteriorates, she will go to live with Pippa's sister and her five children. Until then Pippa, who lives in the same road, pops in to help her mother every day.

'Mum and I were in the room when dad died, and I think it crystallised some kind of closeness between us from then on. And since she's been ill we've got closer. The relationship's become more equal, because the side of her nature that's very domineering has been diminished; she's a weaker person now, and she's more compliant. I don't have to battle with her any more.

'It's hard to say what the future will bring; it varies so much with Parkinson's. Some people die quickly, others drag on in a bedridden state for years. At the moment I should really go in every day to see how she is, and do her shopping; she can't walk very far. The prospect of having to look after her is a burden, and it's worse because I had a child at such a young age [17] so I haven't really experienced adulthood without some kind of responsibility. Normally you'd have young kids and then there would be a gap before your parents needed you in that way. She got ill pretty young [she is 69], and that's the way it's worked out; I'm not going to have freedom in that respect for a long time.'

Diane, whose mother suffers from a form of dementia, feels that the illness, combined with events in her own life, has brought an end to the distance which always existed between them. It has also given her an insight into her mother's life. 'I'm closer to my mother now. She's in a nursing home. After my father's death I began to understand some of the pain she had experienced even in her childhood. That, the death of my father, the pain I experienced myself with the relationship with my husband, and acquiring new knowledge about my own daughters, made me start to think that some of my mother's behaviour was not her fault. I had always blamed her but then I started to understand her.

'I was the only daughter who took the time to kiss her. I do it more now when I see her, I'm more emotional with her. I tell her I love her and I think that's what she's wanted all her life. In her present state of mind I can say "I love you, mom" and she comes back to life. The first time I did that I thought, this is the key to my mother — she's wanted to be loved and she never thought anybody loved her.'

Diane had a quite different experience of role reversal with her youngest daughter, Sarah, which also brought mother and daughter much closer. Diane was in a desperate state when she separated from her husband, and Sarah offered sustained support in spite of the fact that the situation was very difficult for her too. At 16, Sarah was very young to come up with the goods; but if she hadn't, she says, 'I don't know what would have happened to mum.'

Sarah was about to take her Highers (the Scottish equivalent of A Levels) when her parents separated, and she and her mother went to live in a tiny bedsit in Glasgow. Diane remembers: 'The thing that drew Sarah and I together most closely was my marriage breaking down. Sarah came to live with me, although she was not made to. She had stayed with her father for about two months and then they had a row which was the trigger. We lived together in a rented, furnished bedsit and slept together on a pull-out sofa. She didn't have any of her own things — her treasures, her posters — around her, and we didn't have a telephone. There was just a payphone in the hall which didn't take incoming calls, so her friends couldn't call her. It wasn't the sort of place where you could invite friends round, because there was nowhere to be private.

'I became increasingly ill. I wasn't coping, I wasn't working, and I became very depressed. The roles reversed and Sarah was a very caring daughter. I wouldn't say I stopped being her mother, but suddenly at the age of 16 Sarah had to become quite mature and aware of her mother's disability. It bonded us like glue.

'Sarah never spoke about her feelings, but there was an

inner hurt. I was aware of it, and I did the best I could for her. Everyone wanted Sarah to talk but she wouldn't talk out her feelings, not even with me, so I never knew how she felt, except I knew she wanted to be with her mum.

'I was so angry about the situation, not for myself, but for Sarah: for the deprivation and the embarrassment it caused her at school. That brought us close, and though I'm back living with my husband it's an unshakable bond between Sarah and myself that will never go away. I think we'll always remember that time together through the mutual suffering that we went through. I think my husband is angry about the closeness, I think my other daughter is angry about the closeness we share. But it's something that happened to us.'

Sarah's response to the crisis was pragmatic: she concentrated her energies on keeping her mother's every-day life going. Oddly enough, she does not look back on this difficult period as altogether unhappy, largely because of the intimacy it brought. As a child, she had assumed that her elder sister was the favourite: 'She had all these blonde ringlets and there are endless photos of her as a baby. The only ones of me are with her. This changed when we were teenagers, particularly when mum and I moved in together. The only way to live at such close quarters is to get on, otherwise you'd kill each other. I'm sure we had fights, about what to watch on TV or me leaving the flat in a mess, but that's not what stands out about that time.

'I was very aware that my mum was really unhappy. I had to make a conscious effort not to look miserable, par-ticularly since we were living in one room. In a house you can get away and be miserable in your own room; there that was impossible. I used to buy mum the odd bunch of flowers or something when I'd been into town, but I didn't want it to be obvious that I was trying to jolly things along.

'If I hadn't been there I don't know what would have happened to her. I think she would have got very depressed. We used to go shopping or out somewhere which stopped her just sitting at home in front of the tele-vision. It meant she had to get on with everyday life.

'The worst thing was friends at school; I only told a few people what was happening. I stopped going out and seeing friends because I couldn't have people back and because they couldn't get in touch with me. It meant that I worked much harder, though that was difficult at times because I would lay all my books out on the kitchen table and when mum came in to cook I'd have to get rid of them.

'Some of my friends might not understand the situations I've been through, but mum does. I'm closer to her than anyone.'

Sarah's support also proved invaluable when Diane's eldest daughter, by her first marriage, had an accident which paralysed her from the waist down. Diane remembers the visit to the hospital in New York, where Monique lives, at Christmas time in 1987.

'Sarah came to the hospital with me at one point; it wasn't my first visit. I think it must have been very difficult for her. It certainly was very painful for me to see my daughter in that state. Sarah didn't show any outward signs of being upset. When I first told her about the accident she cried; it hurt her a lot, but when visiting in New York there were no tears. I was really grateful for Sarah being there. I had my own sister with me during different visits but it took a lot of pain away to have Sarah with me. Again, she relieved a burden that I had to deal with.'

It can be very hard to turn down a plea for help, particularly if it comes from your mother. Yet it's something many women have to learn to do in order to preserve their own sanity. Some women just can't do it, and struggle on, juggling demands from different directions. Others, like Maureen, who has a demanding family of her own, try their best to maintain a distance. But by doing so, daughters like Maureen court the disapproval of family and friends.

When Maureen's father died last year, she found herself caught between the demands of her mother, who had major heart surgery two years ago, and those of her three children, including her teenage son Mitchell, who has severe brain damage. Her mother's dependence came like a bolt from the blue: 'My mum is like my daughter,

Maxine, she's always been very hard. She never cracks under stress, it doesn't matter what you tell her, she's the same. And I thought that after my dad died, she would get up and carry on and try and enjoy herself a bit. My dad was one of the old school: You're my wife and you'll stay in and do as I say sort of thing. But she's gone the opposite way; she needs me. And she's never needed anybody. It's a bit of a strain because I'm taking her out for a drink every night. I'm trying my hardest not to get any more involved, like taking her out shopping and things like that, because I want her to try and do that herself. Because with having Mitchell I haven't got that much to give.'

Maeve, a single parent in her late thirties, with two teenage daughters, found herself in a similar situation when her father died suddenly. Stifled by the demands made by her mother on the one hand and her two teenage daughters on the other, she made a positive decision to break the pattern she felt she had brought on herself. 'I made the mistake of being available for my mother far too much after my father died and since she regularly has breakdowns it really became incredibly burdensome. I felt torn between my responsibilities for my kids and what my mother and all her relations seemed to see as my responsibilities to her. That's been a very conscious disengagement. At times she's been really angry. When I was in hospital in the summer she never once came to see me; she phoned and told the nurses she couldn't come because her feet hurt and things like that. She'd say huffy things like, "You were ill last year and you're ill again this year." I think it's been quite good for her, because she's starting to get herself together.

'It's been part of a process of knowing more about myself and my tendency to get sucked into colluding with people like my mother who always relies on me like an old brick. Other people depend upon you being the cornerstone of their life, so it's a very big challenge to them, as well as something quite hard to work on in yourself.'

Earlier this year, Gerda decided the time had come to demand support from her two teenage daughters when she reached the end of her emotional and financial tether. Letting down the mask of all-coping mother they had never questioned helped Gerda and her 19-year-old daughter, Rachel, to come to a new level of understanding, based in reality rather than on some ideal image of motherhood.

'It's only recently that Rachel has realised just how upset I can be. Before I used to put on this cold front. I didn't want to tell the children because I felt removed from them in one way, and anyway they were going through their own troubles. Now Rachel knows that mum does cry. That's another thing that's brought us closer together, me letting go and not being ashamed to show that I've got emotions and that things do depress me something awful.

'A couple of weeks ago I got a letter saying I was being taken to court again; this was the one that broke the camel's back. I got in such a tiz about it, and I cried and let off steam and Rachel was very comforting. She made me realise that we had been there before and we'd coped, so we'd cope again.

'I think if I hadn't switched off I would have gone to pot. I did take to the bottle at one time. I'd just started to drive and I'd take the car out, buy a bottle of wine, go to a car park, drink the whole lot and sleep it off in the car. It was the only way I could release tension and was able to cope. That's when I started smoking again, it was just another way of coping.'

Rachel remembers the impact of the dramatic change in her mother's behaviour: 'When my mum started crying and letting go, I just couldn't believe it. In a way I'd put my mum on a pedestal: she was perfect, she coped with any situation, she was cool, she was calm, and that was it. I was so jealous of her being able to cope; I wished I could be like that. Then I thought no, she can't really be like that, she must be really hurting inside, it must be really awful. Up until these last couple of months I didn't realise how it did eat away at her, but now I know nobody can hold that much in.'

10.
ESTABLISHING AN EQUAL FOOTING

'It did seem to be quite a good relationship, but it was all based on a kind of deception, of me performing the role I knew she wanted, of me being someone I wasn't.'

Pippa

'If you talk to a friend about something personal, you never know if they're going to judge you. Whereas I know my mum would never judge me. She can take an outside look as well as an inside look.'

Rachel

There are so many factors militating against satisfactory relationships between mothers and their grown-up daughters that it's surprising that they ever exist at all. Bad habits on both sides — daughters lying to evade disapproval, mothers making devious demands by an excess of self-sacrifice — can be hard to break.

And it's not just a question of the mother accepting that her daughter is an adult. Daughters, too, have to recognise their mothers as individuals, not dictators tied to the kitchen sink whose sole purpose in life is to nurture their children. Too often this realisation, which often dawns when daughters become mothers themselves, comes too late, when the mother is dead, or the relationship is beyond repair.

Inevitably, the future of the relationship between mother and daughter hangs precariously in the balance when the daughter teeters on the brink of adulthood, and everyone thinks she's grown up except her mother. Even women who were married with children at their daughter's age often find it difficult to accept that she's a fully fledged woman. Of course, there's an instinctive element of protectiveness which it's almost impossible to lose. But lose it mothers must.

Everyone gets the odd twinge of 'Oh, that's my baby' when a daughter leaves the nest. Relating to a grown-up woman whose nappies you once changed must be one of the great mysteries of motherhood, and one that is more easily solved by some mothers than others. It's difficult to see a daughter, particularly one on the brink of adulthood, as a real grown-up. As Heather says of her daughter, Joanne, 'I don't find it easy to see her as a grown-up. She's going to be 18 this year, but to me she's nothing near. It's a friendship, but we're also mother and daughter. I don't really feel as though I'm talking to an adult all the time. I'd hate it if I thought Joanne was staying at home because I'm on my own. I want her to have her own life — that's what it's all for, isn't it?'

Diane describes her feelings when she went to see her daughter Sarah off at the airport for a university interview: 'I burst into tears. I thought, I mustn't behave this way but all I could think of was there's my baby going off — it was just terrible.'

Maureen also finds it hard to come to terms with her daughter's adulthood: 'I think now she's 18 it's strange, because I've always done everything for her. When Maxine went to have an abortion recently I was surprised because I didn't have to sign the papers, she did. It's funny, I don't want her to leave the nest. You feel useless — what have you got to look forward to now, sort of thing — your job's done.'

It's easier said than done to allow a daughter her freedom, and more crucially, a separate existence, after years of careful nurture. Jenny, who is 22, remembers, 'When I first left home mum would ring up every day, often first thing in the morning, to check that I was where I was supposed to be. That really irritated me and we ended up having a big row about it. After that she realised I wasn't being as irresponsible as she thought I was and she stopped ringing so often. Now we speak on the phone about twice a week.'

But there are two sides to every story. Roberta, Jenny's mother, puts hers: 'For all her independence, when Jenny was doing a job in the summer she phoned me in tears every day, she was miserable. This is someone who really doesn't want to know you when things are going well.'

Sarah is aware that her mother is anxious about her going off to university. 'You can tell she's worried because she's in such a panic about what I'm taking. She's getting in a terrible fluster about it.' Her mother, Diane, says, 'Sarah's very capable, but she's really bone idle about the house and I do think is she going to have 25 pairs of knickers under the bed, will she manage her money, is she going to revert to the little girl of 12 and find it difficult to make friends. I have a lot of anxiety about whether she's going to get into a lot of heavy drinking, what sort of friends she's going to meet up with. There's a lot of trust that I have to place in Sarah. I just have to let her go.'

Up to this point, Diane has relied on Sarah's awareness that she would be disappointed if she behaved in certain ways, particularly regarding sex. 'I wouldn't be surprised if Sarah desired a sexual relationship — she's 18 — but it concerns me that her current boyfriend is so young. I've told her I don't expect that to happen and I'm trusting her that it doesn't happen. She knows I'd be disappointed. That's the way I put it over, that I'd be very disappointed. I think if she did do it, she'd feel guilty.'

The kind of immediate influence that's possible when mother and daughter live together gets dissipated when the daughter leaves home. From then on it's all down to trust. Every mother hopes that the values she's taught her daughter will continue to hold sway.

But for many daughters, a pattern of deceipt and secrecy established in adolescence, when mother first began to disapprove, can be hard to shake off, even long into adulthood. Some women never feel they can behave in front of their mother as they do in front of their friends. One woman in her mid-thirties told me how deception and lies had become such a habit in adolescent dealings with her mother that it was creeping into adult friendships and relationships, and often thwarting them. She felt that it had drawn her towards sexual relationships where a high level of deceit was necessary; unattached men held no appeal for her.

Jenny remembers the half-truths she used to tell to get round her mother's disapproval. 'There were things I wanted to do that I wasn't sure she'd approve of, so I wouldn't tell her the truth. I used to say I was going to someone's house when I was really going to see someone she didn't like. Or I'd say we were going to Juliet's — which we were — but then we'd go on somewhere else.'

Sally, now 35, deceived her mother in a more far-reaching way as her only means of coping with the very strict rules which her father made, and her mother upheld: 'My mother wasn't disapproving, just terribly, terribly hurt, as if I'd stuck a knife into her. So I would lie to her, because I couldn't bear to hurt her. I could cope with disapproval from my father, but not my mother's hurt. My father used to tell me that I was making my mother have a nervous breakdown.

'I lied to her about everything, where I was going, who I was going with. I used my best friend as an alibi. I wasn't allowed to listen to any music, I wasn't allowed to watch anything except "Children's Hour" on the television, and there were only a few films that my mother would let me go and see, because she was quite strict as well as my father. Wearing trousers wasn't allowed. I've got it in my diary: "My mother's found a pair of my trousers, I'll have to hide the other pair." One thing she knew about that she kept quiet from my father was that I used to go to the Royal Opera House. My father thought ballet was evil, worldly.'

Pippa, who is 29 and has three sons, has always lived very close to her mother: at one point they shared a flat for some years, until Pippa moved into her own flat down the road two years ago. But physical proximity and emotional understanding don't necessarily go hand in hand; in Pippa's case, living together exacerbated her awareness of the gulf between them:

'I know there have been good times and it did seem to be quite a good relationship, but looking back on it, it's a bit sinister in a way because it was all based on a kind of deception, of me performing the role I knew she wanted, of me being someone I wasn't. And there have been all these awful times when she's had a glimpse of the kind of life I do lead — or rather did lead. It was a deliberate deception, I let her believe for several years that I didn't have a sex life. I was frightened by her reaction. It was this thing about failure, that I'd failed her and let her down.

'It's all easier now that I'm settled. The biggest battles have always been to do with sexual relationships that she couldn't understand. When we lived together in London she did try pretty hard. I insisted from the outset that we lived our lives as we wanted to; it was like a flat share and she would just have to accept that. Men still came to see me and we still slept together. It was pretty selfish looking back on it. She didn't like it, but she did accept it. The fact that she was in the flat did put me off a bit; but it was all to do with stubbornness on my part, really.

'But when my second husband came to live with us the worst thing was that I used to feel guilty about going off to bed with him. It wasn't really to do with sex, it was the closeness with somebody, and knowing that she was going to her room on her own and she didn't have dad any more. I felt guilty about being in a good relationship while she was alone. Her whole life seemed to be a struggle from then on. She didn't have dad — they had been pretty close — and she didn't have the kind of companionship that I did. I think I trod all over that really, I didn't really respect what she was going through.

'Getting closer to mum has been to do with having children myself. She can come out with pearls of wisdom that are just to do with experience. She's quite good company now; she's always had a really good sense of humour which is quite a strength. It tends to lessen the pressure.'

This strengthening of the bond between mother and daughter when the daughter's children are born seems to be a common experience. One woman who had refused to speak to her mother for years came round just days after her own daughter's birth: what impressed her was her mother's confidence with the baby.

If nothing else, children give mother and daughter something to talk about, as Yvonne found: 'Since we've had Kirsty my relationship with my mother doesn't appear to have changed, but it does make visits easier because we've now got something we can talk about, whereas before she couldn't understand our lifestyle. We're much better off than they are so we used to avoid talking about where we'd been and what we'd done. And now we've got something my mother can understand and talk about — the family, family life. Visits used to be difficult because we would have the same conversations about Mrs Smith up the road — like mothers the world over — but Kirsty has given the relationship a new direction.

For Angela, a 36-year-old Asian woman, having children has brought increased respect for her mother's views, which used to seem intransigent, like her disapproval of two of her other daughters marrying Englishmen, for example. 'She is an important role model to me now; I wouldn't want to be exactly like her, but there are a lot of good things that she's given me. She never disapproved in a way that made me feel absolute guilt or hatred towards her. It was as if she was distant. It was almost like one look she would give us, but she never said anything, she let us go through it, as painful as it must have been for her she seemed to have kept her feelings to herself a lot.

'Now I can talk about anything, even sex, with my mother, which a few years ago I wouldn't have been able to discuss. Having my own children, having grown up, has made a big difference. You never appreciate anything until you do it yourself; I think my mother was quite brave to go through childbirth five times.

'Initially I couldn't get pregnant for over a year, and my

mum always said, "Well, children aren't everything." When I got really depressed, she'd tell me all the negative things about having children, but at the same time she worried. Any confidences I have I can tell my mum now, and if I want advice I go to her. She's the quiet one, she thinks it out.

'When she used to get proposals of marriage for me, I would rule them out if they lived outside London because I never wanted to be away from her. That's why she laughs that I'm considering emigrating to Australia. I said I didn't want to go because I would miss her. She said, of course we'll miss you too, but if you feel in your heart of hearts that it's good for you and your children then you should go and do it.

'Now I'm a stronger person, I can actually go away from her and still feel that I won't be away from her in soul. And because I am similar to her I feel I can cope with that situation.'

For a happy equilibrium to exist, mothers have to relinquish their control over their daughters' minds and bodies. They also have to relinquish the concept of themselves as superwomen: the all-powerful mother who can set the world to rights.

It has taken Maeve, now in her late thirties, years to come to grips with the guilt she felt as a child for putting an end to her mother's dancing career. Her mother's resentment focused on Maeve rather than her older brother. It's taken a huge effort on Maeve's part to change her own behaviour, and in doing so force her mother to change, so that some sort of equal relationship is established.

'My mother and I never used to talk to each other much before my father died. I feel she resented me from the very beginning. She resented things about me that I had no control over whatsoever, like having curlyish hair and a straight back — stupid things. She was born with a crooked back and her parents took her to specialists and she had to hang on bars and things. It's fairly classic; she obviously wanted a child with a straight back, but at the same time she really resented me. In the same way, she resents my mental abilities, the fact that I can cope with more than she can. And I had a good relationship with my father, we used to have good conversations and she's always going on about how she can't make conversation.

'All my early childhood my mother had gone on and on about how I'd ruined her figure and what a dreadful birth she'd had. I felt racked with guilt as a child for what I'd done to her figure. On top of that, it obviously ruined any hopes she might have had of a dancing career, so there was that struggle going on for her throughout my childhood and adolescence. She was always going into hysterics in my teens about how it was the end of her dancing career and stuff.

'It was quite hard work beginning to have any sort of relationship with her because we hadn't had any before. I think that's the same for her. She's a very trying person to be with. She doesn't listen to anything and take it in, she's very forgetful, and she's got much, much worse as she's got older.

'I didn't really have a sense of myself as separate from my parents. And I find it hard to try and see myself as separate from my daughters, and to get them to see me as someone they should be considerate of. It's something I've worked on with the help of a therapist in the last couple of years, that it's all right for mothers to have needs.'

Recognising that a mother has emotional needs, that they don't just exist to nurture their daughters, can be quite a shock. Some daughters are flabbergasted to discover that not only does their mother have a brain, she's attractive to men — she might even, God forbid, enjoy sex.

A few years after she was widowed at the age of 39, Roberta started to forge her own life. She remembers her three teenage daughters' reaction when she got a place at university: 'They were all amazed and terribly proud. Before that they all used to treat me like a half-wit, Jenny especially.' She also started going out with men. Her three daughters reacted in a characteristically high-spirited, but often embarrassing way; the way Roberta describes it makes it sound like something out of a television sitcom. 'They don't want things to change. They're quite happy about me going out with somebody, but they don't want the status quo to change. They don't want me to move and they want me to be there when they come home.

'They're very critical about the men I go out with. It's almost like a role reversal. They vet people, and they give anyone they don't like a very hard time, Jenny especially. I went on holiday with Jenny two years ago and there was this very nice divorced man on the same table as us. Every time he said, "Would you like to go out for a drink, Roberta?" Jenny would say, "No, she wouldn't." The final straw was when he came down all dressed up for the gala dinner on the last night and Jenny took one look and said, "Oh my God, Medallion Man." He went straight back upstairs and changed. I could have killed her.

'The first man I went out with after Donald died was a bit over the top — large, loud, with a red open-top sports car, white shoes and a hairy chest. I came back about midnight. Before I go to bed I usually check the children. I went into Jenny's room and she wasn't there, then into Alison and Elizabeth's rooms and they weren't there. I was blazing because they were supposed to be babysitting for their younger brother. I went into my bedroom mumbling, "That's what you get, ungrateful children," when the wardrobe door slid open and the girls were standing there saying, "Just checking!" It was so funny.'

The fact that the whole family are able to laugh at a situation which is potentially very tense — the prospect of a stepfather inevitably poses something of a threat — defuses the whole thing. All the teasing and practical jokes may be irritating, but they're also a way of allowing mum to be one of the girls from time to time. It's also a good way of dealing with what Jenny admitted was a bit strange — that her mother was going out more and having a better time than her teenage daughters.

Gill has been forced to reevaluate her relationship with her 70-year-old mother since Karen, the daughter she gave up for adoption twenty-four years ago, made contact with her a few years ago. Gill, who is 41, also has two teenage sons and a 5-year-old daughter, Katy. There are many disturbing incidents in the past which Gill and her mother have never discussed. When she was 16, Gill kept her pregnancy secret from her mother until four days before her daughter's birth; her mother, who didn't acknowledge the pregnancy, says she doesn't remember anything about the events surrounding the adoption.

The appearance of Karen on the scene, and the arrival of Katy, have forced Gill to fight against the reserve which her mother bred into her, and to explore their relationship with a new eye, as much for her daughters' sake as her own. Gill's children — both sons and daughters — have given her an insight into the relationship, and taught her lessons about asserting herself, and to ask questions even if people don't want to answer them.

Yet like many women with elderly mothers, she is wary of causing distress. 'I couldn't look at my mother for months after Karen first rang me. I hated her — I thought, you just don't understand what I've got to go through. At the time [Karen was adopted] I thought my parents would be happy with me, because I was doing what they had wanted. It seems naive now, but I had done that since I was little, I had done everything to be a nice, good little girl.

'I didn't want to push Karen. I never felt I should be dictating to her. I had that sort of relationship with my mother; we're still like that, although mother's 70 and I'm 41. I've been told I don't have a relationship with my mother. I'm struggling with it only to find out more about myself for Karen. I thought, I don't know me, and suddenly I've got another child. Karen has forced me to look along certain roads, whether I want to or not.

'My mother picks on Katy and she picks on me. And I think as a personality I'm inviting it. I'm having to look at my behaviour and think, what part am I playing in this? I ought to stand up to my mother. Both my husband and I are going through this at the moment, learning how to be people with our parents, watching what the adolescents have done before us and trying to be like them so that our parents aren't walking all over us.

'My mother made Easter a nightmare, but I allowed it. I sat there smoothing things over and pretending everything was all right. Whereas somebody should have said, a joke's a joke, mother, but no thank you. Since I've been to the psychologist (which she doesn't know about), my mother says I don't know what it is about you, Gill, but I think you're becoming like your younger brother. He's an alcoholic. He has had fantastic conversations with her about every detail of her life and he's given me the feedback.

'But I don't want her to feel the pain — she's 70 — it might make her ill. As you get older you're thinking on a different level. When you're 20, you don't give a thought to storming off and to hell with the consequences. For me it's getting the odd thing in during a phone call now and again. I don't mean to throw guilt, but there is a little bit of that, and I've got to recognise that.

'My mother has been getting quite hooked on seeing me quite a bit and I was getting quite a bit out of it. Only in the last year have I been offered a cup of tea in her place. She lives in a home for ex-nurses and it's pristine. She would ply me with food and I'd be quite childlike with her. I thought, I can't remember her being like this as a mother when I was a child, so I'm really trying to get to know her. I don't know my mother at all.

'You get an acceptance of your mother as a person. Before, they're the mother who is dictating; you go away and you think, she wasn't too bad. My mother's got some interesting things to tell, if we get away from the stupid domestic things. But it's making the time to get those bits out into the relationship. And that's a question of organisation for all of us — where do we fit it in, how important is it?'

No one could envy Gerda and her daughter Rachel's situation: they're in debt to the tune of several thousand pounds since Gerda was forced to sell her lingerie business, they've been homeless, Rachel suffers from depression brought on by a recent attack of glandular fever. . . . But what is highly enviable is the close bond between them.

'I'm up to my ears in debt, and many's the night I've cried in Rachel's arms, but we've sorted it out, we'll survive. We've formed a strong bond, where when she's down I tend to be the stronger one and when I hit the bottom somehow she's stronger at that time. I don't know how it's happened, but somehow it's really grown over these past two years.

'I made the decision to leave my husband [Rachel's stepfather] and I don't know when it happened, but some time afterwards I realised I needed Rachel and I think that's when I opened up and warmed to her.

'But the transition from the bad times to the good didn't happen overnight — it took about two years. When I divorced, Rachel and I had nowhere to live. We went to a hostel for battered wives, but it was awful, and then we found this place. I think it was when we both realised we were going to be homeless that all of a sudden it started to grow. Now there isn't anything we can't talk about.

'Now Rachel's working at a greengrocer's in Matlock, and I'm struggling to pay off my debts. One lot's going to take 13 years to pay off, the other lot's going to take 28 years. But all these bad happenings have created an extremely tight bond between Rachel and myself, more than between my eldest daughter and me. I wouldn't say Rachel's my favourite, but she's more like me: she's very placid, very easy-going, where the older one is more like her father. She's very quick-tempered and thinks the world owes her a living.

'We formed a bond because we've been through a lot of bad times together; I don't think it will ever be broken. I don't see her so much as my daughter as my friend. We had a similar feeling when she was younger, right up until she started going through this teenage stage when she was 14.

'I think the reason I don't find it hard to treat Rachel as an adult is that I've never been mumsified. A lot of my friends who've had children and have adored them have been utterly lost once they start growing up and moving away. I do have strong maternal feelings, but they're for grown-up children, not for babies. I don't get broody like some women do. I knew that if I was to have any children — which I never wanted — I always wanted little adults. When the two girls were young, I thought, let's get these little years over and done with, hurry up and make them grow up so that I can talk to them and treat them like adults.

'I think that when Rachel had glandular fever she let her frustrations out on me. At the time I was working very hard, often not getting home until 10 at night. That annoyed her, because she could see I was getting so tired all the time. There was friction there, but we got over that. I knew I had to get her out and on the mend, because she was getting very depressed. But she didn't want to do anything, she didn't want to go out. Finally she did and that's when things started to get better. Now we go out weight training twice a week, we go swimming, we go to the pictures, then we have the odd fad — pack up smoking night, twice a year this happens. We sit here and something boring's on the telly, so smoking comes up. We decide to pack up at 6 o'clock, and by 10 we're saying let's go down the pub.'

Rachel says, 'Mum's never shocked with anything I say. If you talk to a friend about something personal you never know if they're going to judge you. Whereas I know my mum would never judge me. She can take an outside look as well as an inside look, which has helped me. Because sometimes I've been so depressed that I don't want to be bothered with anything. At one stage I had to take eight weeks off work.'

Gerda found that time a trying one. 'I was going through a very difficult patch at work. Rachel's depression made her physically ill. I really resented her then, but at the same time I felt sorry for her and I wanted to help her. But I couldn't push through, there was a barrier building. I thought, careful Gerda, it's a similar situation as when she was growing up. I felt she needed help, but I'd given all I could; I hadn't got any more experience to draw from. So I thought she needed outside help.

'I think we've both got to realise that we're both still growing. I'm just trying to prepare her with the philosophy that my gran [who brought Gerda up] drilled into me. I keep saying to her, you're always going to have problems, no matter who or where you are and you've got to solve them as best you can without destroying yourself and anyone else around you. I'm hoping it will give her a grounding for anything that might happen to her when I'm not around — when we're living apart, I mean.'

Rachel feels that she is still under her mum's influence. 'I still look up to her. She's a fine personality, she can be cool when she has to be, but at the same time she can let her emotion show through. We're like each other's shadow, and that's nice. I know there's always somebody there for me. Nothing you can say can embarrass mum or make you feel small. You can be open, it's like talking to one of your friends. I love the relationship we've got and I'm glad she can be as open to me about things as I am to her. Some nights we've been yacking and yacking and it's been two or three o'clock in the morning before we've gone to sleep.'

Gerda feels equally close to her daughter. 'There aren't many people I trust, because I've been done so many times, but if I placed them in order, Rachel would be at the top, my current boyfriend would be second, and a friend would be third. With a friend, you're never quite sure, are you, even if they're your very best friend.

'I see Rachel as a human being, a daughter and a friend, all rolled into one. It wouldn't matter if we were ten thousand miles apart. I know if I picked up the phone and I was desperate, she'd be there if only to listen and to talk. Knowing that is a real comfort. If anybody can say that about anyone else, it's good.'